Otchum,
A Companion in a World of Ice

◄ *Pages 2–3:* Four men, three sleds and 29 dogs crossing central Siberia in the freezing depths of winter.

◄ *Pages 4–5:* In winter the Even use reindeer to pull their small sleds made of leather and wood, which may be used to carry people or materials.

© 1996 Éditions de La Martinière, Paris, France
Graphics and Layout: Rampazzo & Associés
Maps: Éditions Benoît France

Original title: Otchum, chef de meute

© 2000 for the English edition:
Könemann Verlagsgesellschaft mbH
Bonner Strasse 126, D – 50968 Cologne

Translation from French: Andrew Shackleton, Asgard Publishing Services, Leeds, UK
Typesetting: Organ Graphic, Abingdon, UK
Project Management: Transedition Ltd., Oxford, UK
Production: Ursula Schümer
Project Coordination: Nadja Bremse and Birgit Neumann
Printing and Binding: Sing Cheong Printing Co. Ltd.
Printed in Hong Kong, China
ISBN 3-8290-4104-7
10 9 8 7 6 5 4 3 2 1

Nicolas Vanier

Otchum, A Companion in a World of Ice

Adventures of a sled dog

KÖNEMANN

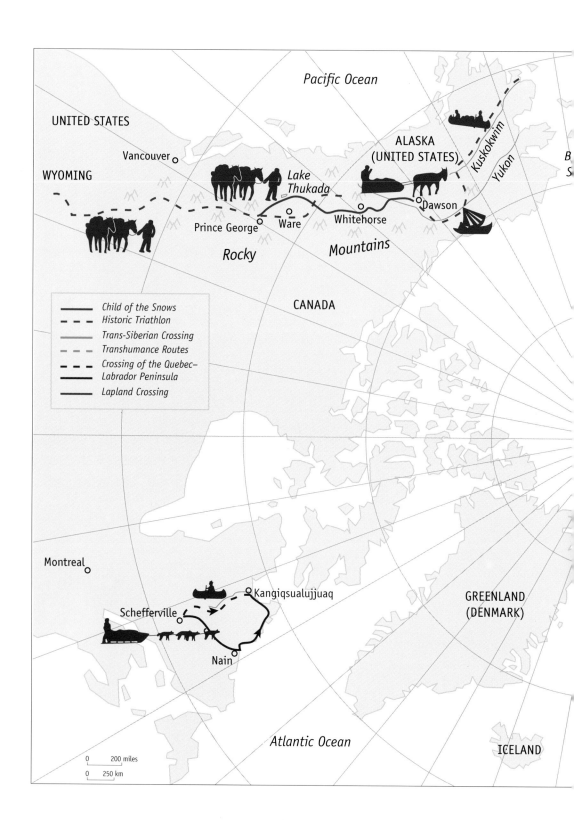

Pacific Ocean

UNITED STATES

Vancouver ○

WYOMING

ALASKA
(UNITED STATES)

Kuskokwim

Yukon

B
S

Lake
Thukada

Dawson

Prince George ○   Ware   Whitehorse

Rocky   Mountains

CANADA

Child of the Snows
Historic Triathlon
Trans-Siberian Crossing
Transhumance Routes
Crossing of the Quebec–
Labrador Peninsula
Lapland Crossing

Montreal ○

Kangiqsualujjuaq

GREENLAND
(DENMARK)

Schefferville ○

Nain ○

Atlantic Ocean

ICELAND

0   200 miles
0   250 km

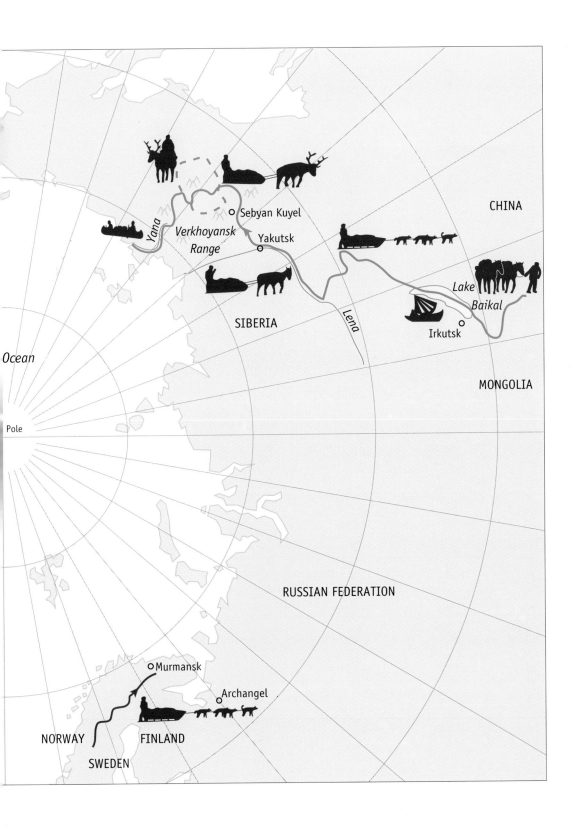

Contents

On the shores of Lake Baikal

When as a puppy Otchum first opened his eyes, he would most likely have seen Lake Baikal – that blue pearl of Siberia, nestling like a jewel amid the encircling mountains. No one could possibly have predicted the amazing career this young dog was one day to have.

Born a hunting dog, it was quite by chance that young Otchum was to become a sled dog, and the only dog in the world to traverse so many frozen expanses: first the whole of Siberia (a record in itself); then Lapland via Norway and Finland and on into the Kola Peninsula; then through the Canadian Rockies and along the Yukon River as far as Alaska – not forgetting hundreds of miles in Europe through the Alps and the Jura. The result has been a record-breaking tour of the world's snowy wastes.

Lake Baikal is a record-breaker too. Not only does it contain the largest volume of fresh water anywhere in the world, but it is home to some 2,600 plant and animal species, three-quarters of which cannot be found in any other part of the world!

It was in a small salmon-fishing village on the shores of this lake that Otchum was born. His name comes from the Russian name for an extinct tribe of people who once lived to the northeast of Lake Baikal.

Otchum must have been born at about the same time that I arrived in the land of the Tofalar, where Siberia borders China, at the beginning of an 18-month expedition across the whole of Siberia to the Arctic Ocean – more than 4,000 miles over mountains, lakes, taiga and tundra, through some of the wildest, most inhospitable, most inaccessible regions of the world.

It took four months on horseback – effectively the whole summer – to get as far as Lake Baikal, traversing innumerable valleys, climbing any number of passes, fording rivers and

◄ Opposite: *Rowing the full length of Lake Baikal – nearly 400 miles in all.*

LAKE BAIKAL

Length: 395 miles (636 km)
Width: 49 miles (79 km)
Maximum depth: 5,315 feet
(1,620 m)

Contains one-fifth of the world's reserves of fresh water.

Is fed by 336 rivers and streams, but has only one outlet: the River Angara, which exits at Irkutsk.

The Baikal seal and the golomyanka, a translucent fish, are just two of the 2,000 endemic species that live in this remarkable ecological niche. Following pollution from pulp mills in the south, the lake has recently been added to the list of the world's great nature reserves in the hope that it can be protected from the greed of today's new capitalists.

penetrating vast swathes of forest.

Arriving at the southern end of the lake, we bought an old fishing boat and rowed for nearly 400 miles to its northern tip. The fresh water was so pure that we could see fish swimming as deep as 100 feet below the boat.

We reached the northern end of the lake at the end of September, and remained there until winter on a small island that lay hidden in a vast expanse of marsh.

Otchum would by then have been about five months old, but we hadn't met him yet. His owner was a trapper who hunted for coypu in the marshes all around us.

In November our thirty dogs arrived by air after an epic journey: by truck from the French Alps (where they had been training for a year) to Charles de Gaulle Airport near Paris, then by airplane to Moscow and Irkutsk, then in an ancient propeller plane to Nizhneangarsk, finally reaching our little island by boat in the middle of a storm!

Because we still needed one or two dogs, we put the word out and the trapper brought us three dogs including the young Otchum. He was just six months old at the time. To make our wait for winter's arrival more comfortable, we had done up a little wooden hut built by fishermen in the middle of the island. Otchum, being the youngest dog on the expedition, was allowed inside the hut, while the thirty dogs that made up the three sled teams were kept nearby.

Winter soon tightened its grip, first freezing the marshes and then covering the whole lake with a thick blue layer of ice as transparent as glass. When we tried out the sled teams on the ice for the first time, we wisely kept young Otchum indoors.

Our teams were perfectly trained, although it was an odd mixture of every breed of sled dog from Alaskan malamute to true husky, Samoyed and Greenlander.

They even included two unfortunate huskies who had been rescued from their Parisian owner. He had bought them when they were two months old – "They're so gorgeous, those tiny furry wolves!" – but had soon decided to get rid of them when, like so many ill-advised dog-lovers before him, he had realized that sled dogs are not suited to walking on a leash through city streets!

Once in the team, these two sad, downtrodden creatures recovered their poise, their energy and *joie de vivre* as they discovered something they had never known before – the pleasure of pulling a sled through vast white wildernesses – which is, after all, what they were made for.

Otchum was not, strictly speaking, a sled dog. He was a laika – a hunting breed selected and trained for many generations by Siberian trappers for chasing wolverine (glutton), sable and bear through the snow. It has been specifically bred for hunting in snow – a powerful athlete with plenty of courage, stamina and intelligence, and capable of dealing with a multiplicity of

▶ Overleaf: *The marshes were so clogged with reeds that rowing was of no use at all.*

DIFFERENT BREEDS OF SLED DOG

Alaskan malamute: This breed is Alaskan in origin as its name suggests, and was developed by the Malamute tribe of Inuit (Eskimos). Being the heaviest and most powerful of the sled dog breeds, it excelled during the great period of polar exploration.

Greenlander: This sled dog, which is slightly less heavy than the malamute, is typical of Greenland and the Canadian Arctic. It possesses the heaviest pelt of any dog, made up of long, thick hairs that enable it to survive the extreme cold and the frequent blizzards of the Arctic.

Samoyed: A primitive breed that is also sweet and very affectionate, the Samoyed is brave and powerful but rather slow. It was (and still is) used for herding reindeer as well as for pulling sleds. It is not, however, a very common breed.

Husky: When people talk about sled dogs, they are most often thinking of the husky. For a long time there has not been a breed of sled dogs as such, and nowadays the classification is rather unclear. And although dog-lovers are becoming increasingly interested in huskies, the various canine clubs around the world have not yet reacted accordingly. Huskies are traditionally thought of as blue-eyed, but nowadays their eyes are more often dark. The husky has generally been considered the commonest and fastest of the sled dogs. But its mongrel cousin the Alaskan has recently overtaken it in speed, and if present trends continue, this upstart will soon overtake the husky in numbers too.

Alaskan: This mongrel breed shouldn't really be included here as it doesn't have any official pedigree, though its lineage has become clearer over the last few generations. The result of careful and calculated cross-breeding, the Alaskan is the Formula One of sled dogs, and is used in about 90 percent of dogsled racing teams. It runs the fastest and achieves some amazing performances, but is no longer a recognizably Arctic breed. The Alaskan is a product of modern times, where speed and performance count but to hell with the rest!

difficult situations such as facing down a bear or a wolverine. Laikas are trained to bark as they pursue their quarry, which they always end up holding at bay, usually up a tree, where they refuse to let them go.

The hunter follows on skis or snowshoes, keeping more or less close to the dog. The dog's barking helps to guide him towards the quarry, which he eventually kills. The chase sometimes goes on for hours and is by no means always successful, as the quarry may take refuge in a cave or burrow where neither dog nor man can follow.

◀ Opposite: *Trappers in Siberia prefer skis to snowshoes.*

▲ Above: *On the small island there was an old fisherman's hut which we restored to provide living space while we waited for the winter.*

◀ Left: *In October winter tightened its grip.*

SIBERIA

Siberia is noted for its extreme continental climate, characterized by massive temperature swings. In the mountains of the Verkhoyansk Range, the temperature may drop as low as –95°F (–70°C) in winter and rise as high as 105°F (40°C) in summer. The Arctic coastal region is occupied by an uninterrupted layer of tundra, which extends for up to 600 miles (1000 km) inland. The rest of Siberia is covered with a coniferous forest known as taiga, apart from a few favored spots where foliage plants grow. In contrast to most of European Russia, nearly all of Siberia's rivers drain northwards. Its great rivers are frozen throughout the winter, and produce spectacular floods as the ice breaks up – a process that begins in the higher regions to the south.

This vast country (nearly one-and-a-half times the size of the whole USA including Alaska) can be divided into three natural regions:

• Western Siberia: a broad plain stretching from the Ural Mountains to the River Yenisey
• Central Siberia: a tilted plateau extending from the Yenisey to the mountains beyond the River Lena (the Verkhoyansk Range and the Aldan Plateau)
• Eastern Siberia: an extremely mountainous region crisscrossed with fold-mountain ranges that become younger towards the Pacific.

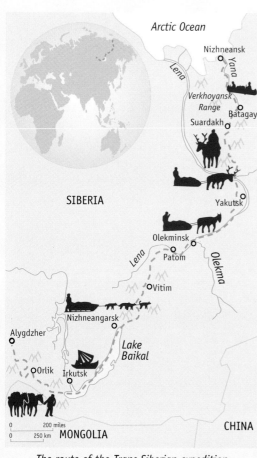

The route of the Trans-Siberian expedition

Running through the snow was an activity that had been almost written into the genes of this young laika, who was a magnificent specimen even at six months of age. But he was still a long way from being introduced to a harness to see if he would accept it and, more importantly, pull a sled.

We tried him out as a sled dog after the first winter snows, which made the slippery ice on the marsh more suitable for a dog to run on. Much to our surprise, Otchum not only readily accepted the harness, but immediately started pulling as if he had been doing it all his life.

"Incredible!" and "Amazing!" were the kinds of words that we used on that day.

The evening after his first outing, Otchum earned a place in one of the three sled teams that were soon to brave the worst of a Siberian winter along a 2,000-mile route at temperatures that would often plunge to below −75°F (−60°C).

Otchum, a laika from the shores of Lake Baikal, had been turned from a hunting dog into a sled dog, and was to become one of those great adventurers that are the stuff of legends.

▲ *Otchum's arrival and our very first encounter.*

Otchum becomes a sled dog

"You're completely mad!" was the invariable reaction of all the hunters and trappers of the Siberian taiga. We were out of our minds to cross this vast, often mountainous territory that stretches from Lake Baikal to the River Lena during the coldest months of the Siberian winter.

"In January the temperature stays between –60°F (–50°C) and –75°F (–60°C) and no one goes out for more than a couple of hours. Traveling in such cold weather, and sleeping outdoors without any heat – why, it's worse than the gulag!"

That last word made it more than clear what the Siberians thought of our enterprise.

But, despite everything, off we went. There were four of us – three Frenchmen and a Siberian (who like me was to complete the whole trek across Siberia) – and of course thirty dogs. There were three sled teams: Jeannot's, Jérôme's and the team allocated to Volodia – a "recovery team" made up of seven dogs, including Otchum.

Volodia and I were supposed to alternate as musher of this team, but given the difficult circumstances I had to spend four months finding the way in front of the sled teams, either on foot or in snowshoes, and resting only occasionally on one or another of the sleds.

At first Otchum stayed in the middle of his team while he learned the ropes: starting and stopping on command, sitting on command, not nibbling at the harnesses or getting tangled up in them, pulling without impeding the other dogs, and saving energy where possible – in short, a crash course in basic sled-pulling skills.

He made quite spectacular progress. From the middle of December, when Otchum was only nine months old, temperatures plummeted to –50°F (–45°C) and then –60°F

◄ Opposite: *The first sled run on Lake Baikal.*

► Overleaf: *Climbing a pass, the trees plastered with snow by the wind.*

OTCHUM

27

► *You often find huskies with eyes of different colors.*

◄ *Nicolas Vanier.*

► *A young Siberian.*

(–50°C). The dogs, despite being well fed, began to lose weight. We had to increase their rations: one portion for work done, one portion for the cold and one portion for general upkeep, which amounted to twice or three times the normal ration.

With them feeding at such a rate, it was vital to keep ahead and reach the first feeding station as soon as possible (we had set this station up before our departure, transporting the food by helicopter to the point we estimated we would reach about three weeks into the journey).

We set off every morning in the dark and traveled on until dusk. The pace was exhausting and became more so as a "certain person" began to sow discord in the group. Dogs and men alike puffed and panted along the icy path, complaining at the effort. Only one of us was happy and that was Otchum – in tiptop form, brisk from the outset despite the cold of the night, and hardly ever tired after each nine-hour battle through the thick snow. He was the only dog to put on weight, defying all the laws of nature.

This expedition should have been much too hard for a dog so young, but far from stunting his growth it seemed to increase it. It was as if, in his effort to succeed, he could draw on all his energy reserves to develop his muscles.

"Amazing!" the mushers kept saying. In effect, Otchum was being conditioned like an athlete.

Day by day I became fonder of this dog with his penetrating gaze and his almond-colored eyes underlined by two white streaks that gave him an air of cunning.

In the evenings I drew close to him in a bid to recover from yet another even harder day that had caused the troops' morale to plummet to rock bottom, just like the temperatures.

MUSHER JARGON

The **musher** is the commander of a sled team of dogs. The word derives from the term "mush," which is the command given for the sled team to set off (perhaps coming from the French Canadian word "marche").

The **lead dog** is, quite simply, the dog at the head of the team. It doesn't have to be (indeed it rarely is) the leader of the pack, who is the "top dog" at the head of the pecking order that exists in every pack of dogs.

The **swing dogs** are those immediately behind the lead dog. They run shoulder to shoulder with him when the team changes direction, and learn the job of lead dog at the same time.

The **wheel dogs** are the pair immediately in front of the sled. They need plenty of strength and stamina, as it is their job to free the sled when it gets stuck, and take the full weight of the sled on their harnesses.

The **team dogs** are all the rest of the team, but no less vital for that ...

SIBERIA –
CRADLE OF THE NORTHERN PEOPLES

The first toolmakers were confined to more southerly climes. It was only about 40,000 years ago, at the time of the last ice age, that the hunters, equipped with warm fur clothing, more advanced tools and the means of heating their dwellings, began to push northward, exploiting the rich animal life of the steppes and tundra. They eventually reached Siberia.

During the last period of glaciation, the sea level dropped sufficiently to link the great continents. The Bering Strait became a bridge between Asia and Alaska, allowing people and animals to migrate westward. But these first migrants had very little effect, as the ice closed off the route southward.

Then about 12,000 years ago a corridor opened through the ice, and the big-game hunters of Siberia finally reached the rich plains of North America.

In January the temperature stayed between –65°F (–55°C) and –75°F (–60°C) both day and night. Otchum was by now ten months old. Always alert, the young laika already sported a broad, strong chest, heavily muscled hindquarters and a tremendously thick black pelt that became white at the front – a magnificent dog.

A few weeks later I insisted on placing him at the head of the team. And immediately, just as naturally as he had taken to being in the team, he took control without the slightest sign of weakness.

He was admittedly content to follow the two teams opening up the trail behind me, but this if anything gave ample proof of his own free will and self-control – in a word, intelligence. Now I'm not one of those people who always tries to turn animals into surrogate human beings, but I am firmly on the side of those who attribute to them a more-or-less rudimentary ability to reason for themselves. The debate is a very old one. Some people think that animals can only achieve two kinds of actions – mechanical and reflex – and that in neither case is any reasoning involved. For such people instinct is enough to explain everything animals do. But I can't agree with this. There are some animals that adapt effectively to new and unfamiliar circumstances for which they cannot possibly have an automatic response. Otchum, like many animals, was capable of reasoning, and to accept this is not, as some people think, a humiliating admission to have to make – quite the contrary in fact.

Otchum was one of those dogs who are destined to be lead dogs – who know how to obey and interpret the musher's commands, but are equally capable of overriding them when the circumstances dictate. He was a dog with a real sense of responsibility.

◀ *Huskies, like wolves, howl in packs, especially at nightfall.*

▶ Overleaf: *A sled run along the shores of Lake Baikal.*

Otchum quickly demanded his place at the front. It was as if he felt constrained by his harness and needed a little freedom to express himself, and to reveal all the intelligence that his sharp eyes betrayed.

From day to day, and from week to week, in the extreme cold of the Siberian winter, in this frozen land that for three months remained untouched by the sun, our companionship became so strong that with Otchum's help I was already developing secret plans for future expeditions. Otchum couldn't speak, but his eyes expressed far more than the few words the men were now willing to exchange, reduced in the circumstances to only the most essential utterances.

All through this hellish winter that was at the same time fascinating in its severity, the dogs kept up the pace, courageous to the end. As the four-month expedition, which was later to be dubbed heroic, drew to an end, Otchum remained in top form, perfectly proportioned, powerful and muscular – in a word, magnificent.

The dogs returned to the French Alps to enjoy a well-earned rest – all, that is, except Otchum, who stayed with me.

There is a lot still to be written about the two of us. But most important of all, we had become inseparable.

THE MAIN TYPES OF SLED

There are as many types of sleds as there are mushers, because each one has the musher's own personal touch. The most arrogant mushers design their own model which they name after themselves. But in general most sleds belong to one of the following three types:

A **basket sled** is the most commonly used form, though it varies greatly in the position of the "basket" relative to the runners. The basket is firmly attached and the front is more or less rounded to help absorb the shock from

A basket sled

obstacles. If the snow is fairly shallow the friction on the basket is minimal, whereas in deep snow the basket stops the sled from becoming buried. This is the ideal sled for expeditions through trackless wastes.

The **Inuit sled**, which the Inuit call the *komatik*, fares badly in soft snow but is perfectly adapted for the sea ice and hard-packed snow of the Arctic, and also for heavy loads. It is normally used with sled teams harnessed in a "fan" formation.

An Inuit sled

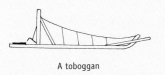

A toboggan

The **toboggan**, the runnerless sled developed by the Native Americans, is perfect for forests and deep snow, which it "surfs." The main drawback is its large area of friction, which slows it down especially when it is carrying heavy loads.

Otchum with the Yakut ponies

In winter the River Lena freezes into a solid highway, which is used by pony teams and a few trucks as they move on from village to village.

In order to reach the foot of the Verkhoyansk Range, which we planned to cross with a team of reindeer, we opted to follow the peaceful course of the frozen Lena, replacing the old dog-sled team with a new team of ponies.

March came, and the sun finally returned to the land of the living. This, together with our new travel companions, brought welcome relief from the unbearable tensions that had built up over the preceding months.

We departed in a festive mood, with Otchum at the head of the party, full of joy at being allowed to run free across the frozen surface of the river.

The team now consisted of five adorable ponies, each one drawing a traditional wooden sled. They were tied together with leather straps that we somehow held onto while perched on top of our equipment.

The ponies kept up a good pace, and we covered between thirty-five and fifty-five miles a day depending on the distance from one relay point to the next. The whole course of the Lena is punctuated by ancient staging posts, the distance between them calculated according to an average day's march for a good pony team. Here the travelers of yesteryear sought food and lodging, and perhaps even a change of mount.

These staging posts have long since given way to villages or farms, and only rarely have they been totally abandoned. Where this was the case, we put up a tent and the ponies found enough dry grass beneath the snow to feed themselves.

Otchum ate up the miles with an immoderate appetite, covering as many as three or four times the normal distance as he ran from side to side across the river, playing and chasing the whole day long. If he became out of breath after a particularly long chase, he would jump onto one of the sleds and cadge a lift for a few minutes before running off again with renewed vigor. The friendly ponies accepted him with parental affection, and gave him full rein as he scampered between their legs and onto their sleds.

Otchum became a source of great pleasure. You should have seen him clowning about, running, playing and yapping with pleasure as we tried to push him off the sled that he was trying to get onto.

Having for five months experienced the difficult world of a sled-dog pack, where his initiative and self-expression had been sorely tried, Otchum was now developing the qualities necessary for dealing with the variety of situations that we were faced with every day.

It was incredible how he could face down the dogs he met in the villages. By the age of twelve months, Otchum was already showing qualities of leadership. It was quite a sight to see with his ears turned back, his fur bristling, his lips drawn back across a magnificent set of teeth, his chest extended and his head held high – a formidable presence that made the villagers whistle with admiration.

As for the dogs, they refused to confront him given the often unexpected nature of his attacks, which were speedily and skillfully accomplished. Most dogs were satisfied with trying to intimidate him, and spent a long time with the preliminaries, sizing him up, then growling and barking while running in a wide circle around him.

Occasionally one dog, slightly more rash than the others, might bare his teeth and Otchum would immediately pitch into him, taking full advantage of the element of surprise. He soon had the upper hand among the village dogs, though we had to remain extremely vigilant, since several times he narrowly avoided mortal combat with some of the more war-hardened dogs and with organized packs that would have torn him to pieces if we had not intervened. But he quickly learned from

every fight in every village, and was soon highly skilled in the art of confrontation.

Another consequence of this, we learned as we moved from village to village, was that he quickly turned into a kind of canine Don Juan. Not one bitch in heat was immune from his attentions, even at the cost of two or three fights with potential rivals.

On several occasions one of the villagers (usually a trapper) brought a bitch forward especially for him to mount. Otchum was eager to oblige, with the result that along the banks of the Lena the number of pups sired by him would soon be counted in dozens!

Hardly more than a few days after we had set off with the ponies, Otchum adopted the role of guardian, preventing any creature on two or four legs from coming near our ponies or equipment. In his mind he had taken full possession of everything that we had, from the snow shovels to the sleds.

You should have seen him, resting on one of the sleds or in any position that gave him a good all-round view. From here he

▲ The Siberians, like all northern peoples, drink an enormous amount of tea.

▶ Overleaf: The banks of the Lena are dominated by massive rock formations like these if possible.

OTCHUM

◄ Pages 42–3: *This Siberian takes his bear with him from village to village. Hunters pay him to introduce their dogs to the bear as a way of teaching them to cope with danger.*

would guard "his" property with the same haughty, condescending look that he reserved for all such occasions.

Another dog only had to raise its nose to Otchum and he would draw back his chops to reveal an impressive array of teeth, ready to return the intruder to where he had come from if a growl should prove an insufficient deterrent.

So at night we could sleep soundly, safe in the knowledge that no one would risk stealing a pony or a rifle. The latter was an object much coveted by the Siberians, forced to rely on the Kalashnikov – an effective but scarcely practical weapon.

Everyone we met, whether in villages or on farms, welcomed us like visitors from another planet. Being the first foreigners (and French ones to boot) to have entered their land, we became a kind of physical symbol of the advent of perestroika. The opening-up of Russia to the outside world was much spoken of in distant Moscow, but its effects were as yet scarcely perceptible out here in Yakutia, thanks to the 3,000 or more miles that separated these two very different worlds. The people were all the more dumbfounded because there was nothing visible to betray our true identity – whether our mode of transport, our equipment, our clothes or even our dog, who was Siberian through and through. As we entered each village, nobody noticed us particularly – we were just another pony team like all the others.

When the villagers found out who we really were, we could see the disappointment in their eyes. They would have preferred to have seen us arrive looking like true aliens. They would eye us suspiciously – could we really be French?

They would then ask us to show them our passports and to speak French, so as to provide irrefutable proof of our foreign identity.

"They really are French! They've come from France!"

Only then would the celebrations begin. Out came the vodka, the pony fat, the pony sausages and the fermented pony's milk. In these parts everything comes from the pony. Every household celebrated our arrival as we passed through, clinking their glasses with a resounding "Na zdorovye!" ("Good health!").

It was in one of these villages which we visited that Otchum celebrated his first birthday.

"Let's drink to Otchum!"

He received a massive joint of meat to mark the occasion. Little did he know that he would soon be presented with a yet more substantial present – several hundred tons of fresh meat that was still running around!

▲ *On our travels we ate plenty of ptarmigan.*

Otchum and the reindeer herd

Otchum was first and foremost a hunting dog. It was his calling, his passion – it was in his blood. This gave us good reason to be worried. What would happen when he met our new team of reindeer – the ultimate big game? It would be like teaching a cat to leave the mice alone!

Around April 1st, after we had arrived with our ponies at Yakutsk, the capital of Yakutia, we had an appointment with the Even and their reindeer somewhere in the foothills of the Verkhoyansk Range. But the question was how to find this "somewhere" in these mountains, given that they extended some 200 miles east from Yakutsk. The Even were playing quite an April Fool's joke on us!

We started to look for them, aiming for a small village of pony breeders and sable trappers over sixty miles from Yakutsk, where several hunters had met "our" Even together with their reindeer a week earlier.

"We almost fired at them! We've never seen reindeer grazing around here before."

Normally the Even never come down from the mountains, where there is plenty of lichen for the reindeer to graze on. But they had consented to do just that in order to meet up with these strange Frenchmen who wanted to cross the Verkhoyansk Range in the same way they did.

These mountains are wild, inaccessible places that are full of mystery. They have the world record for, among other things, the biggest temperature range, which amounts to 200°F (110°C), rising from –95°F (–70°C) in the depths of winter to 105°F (40°C) at the height of summer.

At the foot of the mountains the Even become restless, searching everywhere for lichen for grazing their 150 reindeer, which means they are always on the move.

◄ Opposite: *Otchum, our watchdog, keeps an eye on our sleds.*

OTCHUM

NORTHERN CURRENCY

At one time everything in the north was valued in terms of beaver skins, so that at the various trading posts established by companies, mainly at the river mouths, the prices of items sold were given in "hairy ones". A gun, for example, cost twenty-five "hairy ones", or twenty-five well-prepared medium-sized beaver skins. Very soon these skins were being exchanged for whisky, brandy, rum and other alcoholic drinks. The introduction of alcohol to the peoples of the far north was to prove the most tragic aspect of the fur trade. It was the beginning of the end for them – a process that is still going on today.

"Carry on northwards and you should find their trail."

So off we went in search of the reindeer herd, taking the ponies with us. Eventually, with the help of a trapper and by the grace of God, we finally caught up with their trail. The freshness of the reindeer tracks showed that we would soon find their most recent prints – those with the hoofs still in them.

"Tie up Otchum before ... too late!"

Otchum, nose to the wind, was off like a shot, following the scent. The hunt was on, and the only thing missing was the sound of hunting horns.

Otchum was in his element. The reindeer scattered to the four winds, with Otchum barking loudly in hot pursuit. The Even, enraged, looked for a rifle to kill the wolf.

What an introduction! When you meet a people so full of aura and mystery as the Even, you want to present yourself in your very best light. There was absolutely no chance of that now!

"Hallo, it's us, the French."

"We were expecting you."

"We were looking for you."

"At least your dog found us!"

All of this spoken in something approximating to Russian but no less comprehensible for that!

It took four hours to round up Otchum and the reindeer. Fortunately he hadn't killed any of them, being content to follow them while barking all the time.

To get him used to them, we tied him to a tree at the edge of the clearing where the Even had just assembled their herd. Otchum and the reindeer just eyed each other.

His eyes shone with lust and greed, while those of the reindeer simply bulged with fear. You could practically feel the tension in the air.

After an hour everyone started to relax again. The Even were good sports and were soon laughing uproariously. The whole thing was a mess, admittedly, but they would have a good story to tell their families when they saw them. And to the Even a good story is like gold dust – or rather its equivalent in cartridges, because gold isn't actually worth very much in this part of the world.

The next day we set off for the mountains. The Even, just like sailors on land, start to feel uncomfortable when they are down in the valleys.

"It's like being down in a cellar," they say, "where even rats wouldn't live."

The Even need the mountains like a fish needs water.

Later on I showed a picture of Paris to one of my Even friends and suggested taking him there some time. I was frankly astonished by his reply:

"If we climb to the top of a tower block, we'll be able to see the whole city."

Our departure on reindeer sleds remains among my most treasured memories of this remarkable expedition across Siberia. Just imagine 150 reindeer pulling twenty sleds in single file, snaking through the forest like a vast serpent – there's nothing quite like it for power and speed!

So that Otchum would not panic the herds, I tied him to my sled with a rope, which I soon slackened as I could see he was becoming bored with the crowds of reindeer that moved around him all day long.

He managed to integrate with the herd just as easily as with the ponies previously. It seemed he could adapt to anything.

"What transport method will we be using next time?" he seemed to be asking.

With the ponies we had covered more than 100 miles, while Otchum must have clocked up at least double that amount. With the reindeer we had to travel more than sixty miles a day in order to reach the distant land of the Even. But Otchum's enthusiasm knew no bounds, and he soon became a practiced long-distance runner.

▶ Overleaf: *In winter the Even set out across the tundra with their reindeer herds. They are known as the nomads of the north.*

THE EVEN

The Even and the many other peoples of northern Siberia (a total of twenty-six small nationalities with a combined population of some 158,000) live from traditional activities such as hunting, reindeer herding, and river and sea fishing.

The Even are particularly associated with the mountains of the Verkhoyansk Range, where they have developed a way of life perfectly suited to the harsh and difficult conditions of this region, using the limited resources that it provides.

Reindeer herding remains the chief activity of this northern people, but depending on the season the Even also practice hunting in winter and fishing in spring. They have learned how to protect their environment, to graze the reindeer, and to hunt and fish, in the most effective way possible by means of transhumance – migrating vast distances every year in clans made up of several families.

The nomadic Even use their reindeer while on the move, either as beasts of burden (carrying backpacks or pulling sleds) for transporting goods and chattels (tents, for example), or to provide food and clothing. They make tools out of the skin and antlers, and use the tendons for binding. Even today, reindeer herding still constitutes a major part of the northern economy. In areas where it is still important, it can represent up to 80 percent of total revenue.

"He's quite amazing, that dog," said the Even, who were after all very familiar with laikas, which they use for tracking bear and sable.

Daily, my fondness for this extraordinary dog grew. We could communicate by just looking at each other. He quickly adapted to any change in the way we lived, and always found his place.

By the time we had been with the reindeer for just three days, he had already learned all the commands used by the Even for controlling their animals. He always knew in advance when the herd was going to set off, change direction or stop.

"He's a cunning creature, that one!" said Alain.

He soon became a skilled hunter as well. We no longer had to feed him, unless for our own personal satisfaction as we sat around the fire of an evening. Whenever he got hungry, he could always catch a hare or a few ptarmigan.

At a stopping point we would occasionally catch him with his head cocked, his eyes alight and his nostrils flared. He would prick up his ears, listen attentively, and then, as if obeying a command that only he could hear, he would bound into the forest and launch himself on the trail of an animal he had scented.

He often returned from the chase with his lips still covered with fur and blood, yet with an air of total innocence that made us laugh.

For Otchum it was a time of perpetual fun and enjoyment, forever hunting and chasing across these wild mountains. And it was a great time for us too.

The further we traveled, the more convinced I became that this dog's destiny and mine were forever entwined. How could it be otherwise? I could no longer imagine life without him. As I sat on the reindeer sled, crossing the vast white expanses of the Siberian Arctic, I began to make new plans for future expeditions.

We had been traveling like this for about a week, plunging ever more deeply into the mountainous heart of the Verkhoyansk Range, when we arrived at the Even village of Sebyan Kuyel. We would have to change team here yet again in order to move on towards the source of the Yana, one of the many rivers that empties into the Arctic Ocean – the final goal of this long and difficult mission.

At this time of year, the Even move with their reindeer up into the high mountains, where there is plenty of lichen for the reindeer to graze on. Nikolay, a clan leader and the owner of some 2,000 reindeer, was moving his herds towards the source of the River Yana, and proposed to take us with him. He became one of my best friends, and for four months we were to share intimately in the life of his nomadic family.

Even when the herd wasn't on the move, there was still plenty of work to be done: keeping a 24-hour watch on the herd, hunting and fishing for food, pitching and breaking up

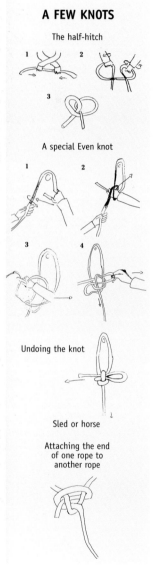

A FEW KNOTS

The half-hitch

1   2

3

A special Even knot

1   2

3   4

Undoing the knot

Sled or horse

Attaching the end
of one rope to
another rope

camp, whether for a day or for a week depending on how often we needed to move.

Never had the word "freedom" meant so much to me as during those long weeks of wandering through the mountains. Life passed quietly and peacefully.

Otchum followed me around like a shadow, exulting in the first rays of the spring sun, which felt all the more welcome after ten months of winter. He spent many hours stretched out in the sun, lazily observing the herd as it moved slowly from one pasture to another.

As the snow disappeared, the reindeer sleds gave way to saddles with backpacks.

After several months of dawdling, it was now time for us to resume our journey northward, always keeping faithful to our motto: "All you gain when traveling is the time that you have lost along the way."

▶ *After ten months of winter, Otchum discovers the pleasures of swimming in open water.*

On the backs of the reindeer

For the summer migrations we had to load all the equipment onto the backs of the reindeer using backpacks made of leather. Otchum could have had a backpack too. At one time the Inuit used to transport their most vital equipment in bags tied to the backs of their sled dogs.

But Otchum had already pulled a sled during the winter, and it was so much fun to watch him capering about the tundra that I didn't have the heart to make him carry anything. Besides, there was no need when we had 2,000 reindeer to do the job.

Otchum had become well integrated with the dogs belonging to the clan – or rather the dogs had quickly acknowledged him as leader. Not that they could have done otherwise, as Otchum was the biggest and strongest in every respect – size, weight and musculature, not to mention energy and endurance.

Nikolay, the leader of the clan, was stubborn by nature, and not a day went past without him repeating the same request: "Leave your dog with me when you finish your journey. He won't be any use to you in France."

In my rather inadequate but nonetheless comprehensible Russian, I invariably told him it was out of the question, upon which Nikolay would retreat, laughing and joking: "This Nicolas is even worse with his dog than Sergey with his fiancée." And everyone in the clan would laugh uproariously, casting envious glances at Otchum.

At this point in the expedition I was alone with the Even. The three Frenchmen who had been with us throughout the spring had returned to France, while Volodia had joined them in the helicopter that had come to fetch them, in order to see his wife in Yakutsk.

Otchum and I spent long days wandering about the tundra, searching for the fish and game that formed the major part of

◄ Opposite: *Volodia, my Siberian companion for the whole of the Trans-Siberian Expedition, is a geologist by profession and a passionate explorer.*

our diet that summer. Otchum would drive out the hares onto the bushy slopes and I would kill them as they tried to escape. We were happy to share the spoils between us.

Otchum was less happy with wolves. He no doubt hated them as much as the Even did, for they couldn't speak about wolves without spitting on the ground. Every spring the wolves would follow the herd and wreak havoc among the fauns. The Even took it in shifts to form a 24-hour guard around the herd, but the wolves were very clever and only attacked stray animals. Only rarely did one of the Even actually kill a wolf.

One day Otchum and I went to take up our positions not far from a fresh carcass that had fallen victim to two wolves. They would almost certainly return to finish their meal. Nikolay had instructed me to keep guard and shoot the wolves if the opportunity arose.

I was feeling a little ashamed because, although I hadn't dared admit this to Nikolay, I felt incapable of killing wolves, having just as much admiration for them as the hatred that Nikolay felt towards them. I kept saying to myself that if the worst came to the worst I could always shoot off target. As we approached the area where the wolves had killed three young reindeer, Otchum suddenly became subdued. With his tail between his legs and his shoulders hunched, he was walking just like somebody with tight shoes on, and his eyes seemed to say quite clearly to me, "Come on, let's get out of this place!"

I gently made fun of him and he gave me a look of such misery that it seemed to come straight from the heart. I thought this would do him good, this great fighter who always ended up on top.

I hid behind one of those rocky knolls that you often find in the tundra and that always leads you to wonder how it got there. Otchum lay close to me, trembling imperceptibly. Did he think I would save him from the wolves? We never saw a single wolf, but I'm convinced that one of Otchum's best memories of the whole summer was the moment when, after five hours of lying in wait, we finally left the area.

What is the reason for this ancestral hatred that exists between dogs and their close cousins the wolves? Perhaps the answer has something to do with the wild animal's feeling that domestication is somehow degrading. If a wild animal has been tamed and then returns to its own kind, it will always be rejected and sometimes even killed. Perhaps human odors have something to do with it. But one thing can be said for certain: Otchum never liked wolves.

On the other hand, he simply adored bears. A laika is basically a dog that hunts bears. It's in his blood. Otchum could disappear for hours on end if he crossed the path of a bear. And this happened once or twice in the Verkhoyansk Range, which harbored some rather good specimens.

The Even don't hunt bears, though they might possibly kill one if it became too curious and tried to come too close to the camp or the food supplies.

On one occasion, on our way back from fishing for trout in a lake, we came upon a particularly large bear, which quickly ran away across the tundra. It must have been hunting for lemmings among the lichen. Otchum immediately gave chase, barking loudly after it but always keeping a safe distance of at least 65 feet behind the bear in case it should turn around and attack. The bear stopped to face its pursuer for just long enough to register the ridiculousness of the situation – a "tiny" 70-pound dog in pursuit of a dangerous carnivore weighing some 400 pounds. Otchum stopped immediately but carried on barking. The bear charged but, quick as a flash, Otchum ran away only to stop when the bear stopped. We watched this carryings-on from a distance. They stared at each other for a few minutes, then the bear set off towards the forest at a leisurely trot, with Otchum in hot pursuit. He returned six hours later, exhausted but exhilarated. What a time he'd had!

A bear hunter could have followed the dog on foot or on horseback, guided by the barking, until the bear stopped and

DOG AND WOLF PRINTS

Dog prints (according to speed)

walking

trot

gallop

The difference between a dog and a wolf print

Dog

Wolf

MEDICINAL PLANTS THAT CAN BE USED TO TREAT DOGS

Winter horsetail: once boiled, it alleviates lower back problems.

Wake robin: steep the roots in water, and the infusion will help in the treatment of colic.

Silverweed: grind the leaves or make an infusion from them to treat bruised paws, especially between the pads.

Blueberry: the astringent power of the leaves can prove very effective against diarrhea.

Balsam fir: the gum can be applied to wounds to speed up the healing process.

◄ *This 94-year-old grandfather still does his share of the work, guarding the herd.*

▲ *On an expedition,*
the evening meal
assumes a special
importance.

▶ *The reindeer are*
caught by means of
a lasso so that they
can be mounted,
loaded – or eaten.

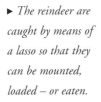

stayed still. He would then have approached silently and killed it. The same technique would have worked for moose (elk), lynx or wolverine (glutton) alike, provided the dog possessed the three essential qualities of courage, endurance and a really good sense of smell. Otchum would certainly have become one of those hunting dogs if our paths hadn't crossed.

We often went high up into the mountains to hunt wild sheep, but we didn't take Otchum with us on these occasions. Hunting for sheep requires a silent approach for which Otchum is not exactly suited. After our first vain attempt at hunting sheep with him, Nikolay strongly advised me to leave him tied up at the camp.

Sheep hunting is one of the Even's most important summer activities. It gives them the opportunity, which is never to be missed, of eating something different from the eternal round of boiled reindeer meat. But how many hours, how many days, of hiking were required, often in vain, just to bring two sheep back down to the camp!

July marked the end of this idyllic period of nomadic life with the Even among the mountains of the Verkhoyansk Range. Otchum and I had an appointment in a small fishing village near the headwaters of the River Yana, where we were to embark by canoe on the final stage of the expedition.

Nikolay agreed to take me there. It gave him an opportunity not only to explore new territory but to add another week to the remarkable collaboration which we had enjoyed over the summer months.

"Come on, Otchum, off we go now! We're leaving the mountains."

Canoeing towards the Arctic Ocean

Summer in Siberia was a blessed time for predatory animals, of which Otchum was one. The young birds, which hadn't yet learned to fly, provided easy prey, while the little leverets could not yet run fast enough to escape. It was a time of rich pickings.

And Otchum did not stint himself. On the contrary, he killed for pleasure rather than necessity, killing a leveret without the least hesitation only to abandon it without even a nibble. This behavior enraged me, and I shouted at him and scolded him for every "murder" he committed. But his instincts proved stronger than my rebukes. Whenever a leveret broke cover in front of him, showing its white hindquarters as it leaped into the grass, he simply couldn't stop himself. He gave chase and caught it. How could he possibly resist the enjoyment of cracking the bones with his jaw, or the taste of warm blood in his mouth?

Wolf cubs will react similarly, killing for pleasure in what is effectively a learning game. Animals have no sensibilities – which is fortunate, given that nature is no fairy tale and can sometimes be cruel. Predators eat their victims alive, while fathers may even devour their own sons – the list is endless.

Otchum needed to learn respect – perhaps not for life in the form of these clumsy leverets and young birds, but certainly for orders such as "No!"

I would try once, twice, perhaps ten times or more – whatever it took until he would finally allow a leveret to escape in front of his eyes.

"Good dog!"

Nikolay couldn't understand this way of doing things. One hundred leverets couldn't make any difference. After all, there were millions of them living in the taiga. "Let him do it if it amuses him!"

◄ Opposite: *We canoed for 750 miles down the River Yana. With daylight for 24 hours a day, the temperatures rose to 105°F (40°C) even north of the Arctic Circle.*

OTCHUM

The Even, like all those who live close to nature, react differently from us towards animals, whether wild or domestic. Domestic animals serve a useful purpose; wild ones provide food and clothing. There's no room for too much sentimentality – and no birthday cakes for dogs!

They don't judge nature, because they are part of it. We, on the other hand, are cut off from nature, and we have such stereotyped, antiseptic images of what is involved – beef steaks wrapped hygienically and laid out in neat, clean rows along the supermarket shelves. We too easily forget that a young bullock had to be slaughtered for this, that blood flowed and that knives cut through flesh.

"No, Otchum!" I shouted yet again, all for the joy of seeing a leveret run free through the taiga.

"Let him do it!" repeated Nikolay, laughing uproariously.

A few hundred leverets later, we arrived in the valley of the Yana. As we gazed down from the mountain tops we were about to leave, Nikolay pointed out a marshy plain covered with hundreds of silvery lakes upon which masses of geese and ducks were to be found.

"The ground underneath these swamps is stuffed with mammoths," said Nikolay. "I've found tusks so large that I couldn't even move them."

"Keep it to yourself," I replied, "or by next month everybody will be coming here."

Nikolay shrugged his shoulders. He thought this area of the planet was much too isolated for the whole world to start visiting. He was wrong.

We descended towards the Yana through extensive forests of pine and birch. At one point Otchum and one of Nikolay's dogs drove a bear out of the cover and ran after it, barking loudly. Their cacophony was soon lost in the forest. One hour later Otchum finally returned – alone. We never found Nikolay's laika again: chasing bears is a dangerous sport.

"What a pity, that was a good hunter" was Nikolay's only comment as we left.

He did not say "What a pity, I liked him."

▲ *We found this mammoth tusk during the course of our Siberian expedition.*

For Nikolay a dog merely served a useful purpose.

After lots of adventures and a few days of walking through thick forests, we arrived at the small village of Suardakh. Volodia, the Siberian geologist who had been with me throughout the Trans-Siberian expedition, had arrived here by plane two days earlier, together with the three Frenchmen who were to take part in this final stage of the enterprise.

Otchum was now to become acquainted with yet another means of transport: the canoe.

Nikolay returned to the mountains after I had promised to spend the following summer with him and his clan. Such a promise would be easy to keep, since by then I could dream of nothing else.

A few days later we set off on the River Yana as it wound its way gracefully through the tundra.

Otchum immediately took up position on one of the two boats – a sort of catamaran made up of two canoes joined together. He stood at the prow like an ancient figurehead, keeping a close eye on everything that was happening on the banks. If a moose (elk) fled as we approached, or a flock of geese flew overhead, he would bark loudly. A hare would just make him growl.

As soon as we came ashore, he would run for shade to escape the heat of the Arctic summer. If we stayed for a long time he would dig down until he found the permafrost, which provided welcome relief. A lot of persuasion was needed to get him to leave his "refrigerator" and return to the boats.

The Siberian summer is a dreadful season, plagued by extreme heat and a heady cocktail of mosquitoes, gnats and horseflies. Otchum was protected by his thick fur, which made his skin inaccessible to mosquitoes, but he still had to hide his nose in his tail. We daubed ourselves with evil-smelling creams, but there was no respite. The sun shone non-stop 24 hours a day, so that the river became a little warmer every day. But its water still remained the only way of escaping both the heat and the insects. Otchum followed the example of wild animals, staying for hours on end in the water.

In the few villages we passed, the inhabitants never took a break. It was a question of garnering everything that nature had provided in the form of fruit, grain or mushrooms during a warm season that was all too short.

Otchum, overwhelmed by the heat, gave up looking for fights and contented himself with guarding the boats, snoozing in the shade of their hulls, having first dug out a trench underneath them.

As we rowed downstream, every stroke brought us nearer to the Arctic Ocean that was the goal of this expedition. New projects were forming in my head, and Otchum was naturally part of them. He was in fact the main protagonist, since whatever I decided to do, I would need my own sled team. I had the father, so all that was needed was a suitable mother for breeding the kind of offspring that would live up to my sled team expectations.

In the village of Kazachye I found out that Amundsen, one of the most famous Arctic explorers, had bought some dogs here that had become the heroes of his extraordinary adventures. According to the Siberians, this village provided the best dogs there were, and we quickly found some excellent stock. These dogs were remarkably well built, thanks to a long pedigree developed by rigorous selection over many generations, in a place where sled dogs were indispensable. I let it be known that I was looking for a bitch puppy some two or three months old.

A whole line of pups was made available for me to view one after another. Otchum came with me, although he was more interested in exploring an unknown village, or in vaguely looking for a bitch in heat, than he was in my choice of a future mate for him. I eventually settled on a magnificent seven-week-old bitch puppy. Volodia, who also wanted to start his own sled team, secured her sister in exchange for a second bottle of vodka.

We left Kazachye with these two adorable little bundles of fur secreted in our coat pockets. I called mine Jana, and Volodia also gave his a name. We were crazy about these two little mascots which had become the objects of our attention.

To our great surprise, Otchum also showed great affection for the young pups, who immediately adopted him, although he was often as exasperated as a mother who has to put up with the cries and whims of a young baby. The pups loved to spend the day climbing onto his back, biting his ears and tail, and scratching his nose with their little claws – in short, annoying him as only a two-month-old puppy can.

We were amazed to see how patiently he bore this. At times we almost pitied him as he looked as though he was being subjected to the worst of tortures. At other times too, though less often, he consented to their games, sometimes even taking full part in them. He would yap and run away, lie on his back while pawing the air, and then charge at the pups just before they caught him. He would nibble at them and allow them to bite him back, then pretend to fall over when one of them tried to push him away.

When we laughed at these antics, he would stop suddenly like a naughty child, and try to resume an air of dignity that befitted his station. We would laugh even more, which annoyed him, and he would wander off to sulk until I went up to him, to whisper affectionately in his ear – "Well, you still have some fighting in you!" – and vigorously stroked his ears in the way he loved best of all.

He would soon return to the pups, who would snuggle in between his paws and his belly. Such tender babysitting was a sight to behold.

A month later the puppies had doubled in size and begun to act like young dogs. They were quite superb, and we never regretted our choice. I was already starting to imagine what their offspring would look like – the color of their fur and eyes – when a tragic accident destroyed all we had hoped for.

Every evening we went into the forest to gather dead pinewood for lighting a fire. September had chased away the summer, and at night the temperature was already dropping to 23°F (–5°C). We were warming ourselves, and the puppies were hidden from sight among the tall grass. Volodia returned carrying a large pine log over his shoulder. As soon as he arrived

▲ Top: *Otchum and Volodia –
the two Siberians on this
expedition.*

▲ Above: *Otchum acts as a
babysitter.*

▶ Right: *The River Yana rises
in the mountains of the
Verkhoyansk Range. It
meanders a lot at first, then
runs more gracefully between
the hills until it finally empties
into the Arctic Ocean.*

at camp, he threw it down onto the ground. The log landed heavily on Jana, completely crushing her spine, and I was forced to kill her to put her out of her misery.

You can imagine the atmosphere that evening. It was horrible. Volodia blamed himself for the undeserved death of Jana: "I should have looked before I threw that log down."

But how could he have guessed that Jana was there when Otchum and the other puppy were playing further away on the river bank? The three were never apart – or at least hardly ever.

That very evening, Volodia suggested that I should have his dog instead.

"No, Volodia," I said, "it's your dog, for your future sled team. I have Otchum, so you should keep her. Thank you all the same."

We soon arrived at the Arctic coast, but nowhere among the coastal villages could we find a suitable replacement for Jana. It seemed as though Otchum was fated to find a mate in France.

Otchum in Paris

"So, Otchum, we're going back to France." The laika climbed into one airplane after another as if he'd been doing it all his life, without the slightest apprehension.

◄ Opposite: *To celebrate our arrival, our friends had built a raft, which we used to cross Paris.*

It has to be said that in 18 months Otchum had seen airplanes of every color, and had traveled by every imaginable means of transport, from reindeer sled to helicopter, and from boat to military tank. During our visit to the Even village of Sebyan Kuyel, we had been taken to see an old gulag. Our guide, who was one of the heads of the Yakutsk militia, had taken us there in a tank. It had to be seen to be believed!

Nothing surprised Otchum any more – not even Paris, where we arrived by raft on the Seine to celebrate our arrival. My friends had spent a week building this magnificent craft – a copy of the raft we had built for crossing Alaska on a previous expedition, modeled on those of the gold-seekers of the Klondike, made of pine logs with a canvas tent mounted on it. It looked really stylish, floating silently along the silvery waters of the Seine, alongside the Île de la Cité, beneath the arches of the Pont de la Concorde, and close to the Eiffel Tower, while cars passed slowly along the embankment expressway. That evening, TF1's eight-o'clock news gave us images of Otchum, the new star. The next day he appeared on the front page of France-Soir, and a special television appearance quickly unleashed a media avalanche. I had decided to broadcast the fact that I was trying to "marry him off," so it wasn't long before dozens of sled-dog owners were offering their bitches as mates for the famous dog.

Meanwhile, far away from all the media hype of the city and all its excesses, Otchum soon came to love the Sologne region, to the south of Paris, where we lived on a farm several miles from the nearest dwelling.

Otchum took full part in everything we did: traveling by boat, fishing for pike, working in the woods and fields. He

▲ Above:
Ska, the Greenlander, with her first litter.

▶ Right:
Otchum arrives in Paris.

▶ Right:
Baikal.

▶ Right: *Otchum on a frozen pond in Sologne.*

DOG TRAINING

Among the dog owners of the far north there are two schools of thought as to the best season for bitches to have their litters. Some think the pups should be born in summer, others in winter. One group says that pups born in winter will be stronger, because they will get used to difficult conditions from a young age.

The others think pups have a better chance if they are born in summer, because this gives them a better chance to develop properly.

My own personal opinion, culled from long years of experience, is that pups should preferably be born at the beginning of summer, not only because it gives them the best chances for their development, but because they can then start training in the middle of winter, at that key stage in their development between the ages of six and twelve months.

always tried to make himself useful, diving into the water to bring a duck back in his mouth, and even plunging through thick bushes to drive away a herd of wild boar who were devastating a crop of Indian corn.

My quest for a mate for Otchum led me to Louis Bavère, who was one of the first Frenchmen to have owned a team of sled dogs, long before the idea ever became fashionable. He used to breed Greenlanders for a magnificent team made up of dogs of genuinely northern pedigree. Such hefty specimens were capable of pulling a heavy sled through deep snow at temperatures below −60°F (−50°C). He would never consider huskies, which had increasingly been bred for speed ever since the mushers had introduced competitive sled racing in 1985.

Louis suggested a young golden-eyed bitch called Ska. Otchum accepted her immediately, and with all the more enthusiasm because she was coming into heat. The "marriage" was quickly consummated. Otchum was then moved to the Jura mountains to be cosseted by Jérôme Allouc, who also owned a pack of Greenlanders. There we made good use of the two months of waiting by creating a vast park on the edge of the forest, which was to become home to Otchum's future progeny.

One April evening Jérôme received a telephone call to say the pups had been born – four magnificent specimens, which we named Torok, Nanook, Baikal and Voulk: Torok after one of Louis' dogs which I was very fond of; Nanook after a polar bear I particularly admired; Baikal after the Siberian lake where Otchum had been born, and which we had spent two months crossing in an old fishing boat; and finally Voulk, named after the Russian word for wolf, the animal which I admire above all others.

Otchum must have been the only one to not take the slightest interest in his progeny. Besides which, Ska, as is usual for a bitch, refused to allow him near her pups. She would show her teeth and growl at him, making it abundantly clear she was not joking, and Otchum would retreat.

On the other hand Ska had perfect confidence in us, even allowing us to look after the pups when we took them in our arms. She would use this as an opportunity to take a walk, knowing that nothing could happen to the pups while we were there. She was an excellent mother, providing plenty of nourishing milk, judging from the speed with which the pups were growing.

Baikal was colored black-and-white, Nanook grayish-white, Voulk creamy-white and Torok golden-yellow. They began to squabble and play, passing the whole time nibbling, jostling and climbing all over each other. Gradually Ska allowed Otchum to come closer to them. Occasionally Otchum would even deign to take part in their games, though not with very much enthusiasm.

In the meantime I had managed the same "operation" for myself as I had for Otchum. Marriage had been followed a few months later by a birth. My wife is Diane and we called our little daughter Montaine, after Ste-Montaine, patron saint of the Sologne region.

Diane and Montaine were going to accompany us on our next expedition, as soon as Torok, Nanook, Voulk and Baikal were old enough to pull a sled.

Diane was worried. "Six dogs are not enough," she said. "We need at least ten dogs, which means one or two more litters."

A pack of ten dogs is expensive to feed. But fortunately I managed to clinch a partnership deal with Pedigree Pal. I agreed to test out a special dehydrated high-performance dog food which would later be used to feed the pack during my next expedition.

Pedigree Pal would benefit from the deal in terms of the publicity generated by the media coverage of my next adventure, whether by journalists, writers or movie makers, not

to mention the advantages of having my dogs as guinea pigs for testing out their product.

The dogs grew fast, and everyone agreed how magnificent they were.

"You've been lucky," said Louis. "No one could possibly have guessed the result of crossing a laika with a Greenlander." I was, in fact, supposedly the first person ever to have tried out this experiment.

We wanted to wait for a year before the next litter, but an "accident" decided the matter for us, and four more pups appeared only eight months after the first litter.

One we called Oumiak after a kind of Inuit canoe made of hide and used for hunting on water; the second Amarok after the lead dog belonging to a Native American friend of mine. The other two included a male who died and a female we decided not to keep.

When I went to the Jura to see the new progeny, the dogs from the first litter were already old enough for me to try them out with a harness for the first time. That morning was a time of great emotion.

Otchum, as the lead dog, looked very much the professional, giving his sons a condescending look as they entangled themselves in their harnesses. The result was general confusion, and the process of disentanglement was made all the more difficult by the need to avoid hurting them. God forbid that we should put them off the idea of pulling a sled before they'd even started!

At first the activity was to be treated as a game – a chance for them to have a good run and explore new places – nothing more. It wasn't worth the effort of teaching them things they would be able to learn for themselves as they got used to being in their harness. We introduced the harnesses playfully, praising them all the time. They rolled over onto their backs, expecting us to make a big fuss of them. Once we had attached the harnesses we needed two pairs of hands to keep them going in the right direction, to disentangle the knots and to stop them biting the reins.

"Go, Otchum!"

Otchum remembered everything well. He tugged on his harness and launched himself along the track made in the snow. The four dogs followed him immediately, and were so delighted at capering along the track that they were oblivious of pulling a sled from which Diane and I were giving the orders. Jérôme was out in front of us with his own dogs, providing the kind of competition that northern dogs always respond to.

I was in heaven! Jérôme made victory signs. For a first try it had been an astounding success. The four dogs pulled together beautifully, staying in line and keeping the reins taut, and grunting all the time with satisfaction. We needed to keep them under restraint the whole time to keep them from careering into Jérôme's sled.

I had always dreamed of commanding my own sled team, and now my dream had finally come true, with Otchum at the head of the team.

They looked so much at ease in their harnesses that you might have thought they'd been pulling a sled for months.

"I can hardly believe it!" Jérôme kept saying.

The training now began in earnest. We taught them a few essential commands. "Sit!" was the first one they had to learn – waiting in harness until they were told to go.

"Go!" they learned for themselves. When the lead dog set off they automatically followed.

"Stop!" was more difficult to teach them, especially when they wanted to carry on – this command took them much longer to learn. But the two hardest things they had to learn were getting a paw out of the reins when it got caught, and stopping without getting entangled.

They gradually learned other orders such as "Stay!" and "Positions!" and "Slow!" They were good pupils.

After two months they had become fully fledged sled dogs, working well and enjoying doing it. They seemed to be fast runners, though it was difficult to tell at this age.

SLED TEAM FORMATIONS

Tandem

Double tandem

Fan formation

▲ Above: *Oumiak on her mother's back.*

▶ Right: *Pups are very sociable, always eating, sleeping and playing together.*

▶ Right: *In the forests of the High Jura, the pups were given enough freedom to learn about life.*

▶ Right: *The first litter.*

▶ Opposite: *A man goes ahead on skis or snowshoes, opening up a track for the dogs to follow, which then enables them to save their energy.*

We were less fortunate with the third litter, which included only one male – Oukiok – who had golden eyes like his mother. We couldn't keep the females as they would reduce the effectiveness of the team. It's rather like the crew of a small boat crossing the Atlantic. Take a six-man crew and you're likely to succeed. Add two women and the boat is unlikely to arrive.

It's the same in a sled team – for the dogs to work well they must not be open to any distractions. Apart from the mother, I allowed only one female – Oumiak – into my team. That was just about manageable.

At the end of the winter we all left in a truck, in a party that included both Jérôme's team and mine. Our destination was Lapland, where we were going to cross the Kola Peninsula from Finland to Murmansk. Otchum was to return to the far north and lead his pack there for the first time.

Lapland

There was still one kind of transport that Otchum had yet to encounter – a ferryboat. This was inevitable on a trip to Lapland, which meant a two-day sea journey between Germany and Sweden.

After that we would find the snow we had left behind in the Jura, and this time we wouldn't leave it again. The dogs were very nervous in the truck. The journey was a long one, involving four days of travel by truck and boat. But eventually we arrived. I immediately harnessed the sled team, with Otchum at the front, then Oumiak and Amarok behind him, followed by Baikal and Voulk. Finally at the back, immediately in front of the sled, I placed the so-called wheel dogs – the mighty Torok and his splendid companion Nanook. Our little team was looking good already.

The sled carried everything we needed to take with us for a journey through the forest: a canvas tent, a wood-burning stove, an ax and a saw, a chain for tying up the dogs overnight, sleeping bags and a groundsheet, food for the men and the dogs (two pounds per dog per day) sealed in day packs, a rifle, a first-aid kit and a few personal effects. For a journey of about three weeks, the weight amounted to some 450 pounds (200 kilos) per sled.

As we were setting off we wanted to find out more about the route. We asked a local service-station proprietor, who also owned a herd of reindeer, to show us the best paths. He was the local Finnish businessman, sporting a large nugget of gold hanging beneath his chin.

"The lake is too dangerous, the ice is breaking ..."

"The forest, you'll never find a way through there ..."

"The mountains, they're closed to visitors ..."

We had already checked with the warden of the national park we were about to cross, and she had assured us there was no restricted access. So we treated the man's lies with the

— Route of
Lapland crossing

Barents Sea

Hammerfest○

Murmansk○

Kola
Peninsula

Tromsø○

White Sea

LAPLAND

RUSSIAN
FEDERATI

○Kiruna

○Rovaniemi

Arctic Circle

Bodø○

Luleå○

○Oulu

FINLAND

Atlantic
Ocean

Umeå○

○Vaasa

SWEDEN

Steinkjer○

Härnösand○

HELSINKI▫

Molde○

Lillehammer○

STOCKHOLM▫

NORWAY

Baltic
Sea

OSLO▫

Visby○

North
Sea

○Kristiansand

○Göteborg

0   100 miles

0   100 km

DENMARK

○Kristianstad

contempt they deserved, and set off in front of his very eyes towards the lake he had advised us not to trust.

He was furious, and that very same evening he sent out the national park rangers to check that we were observing the regulations correctly. We gathered that he was saying all kinds of things about us. He was overjoyed when he heard they had confiscated the rifle we had brought for the Kola Peninsula (it was to be returned to us at the Russian border once the necessary permit had been obtained from the Soviet Minister for Foreign Affairs). He was telling everyone that we were hunting illegally, hoping that these evil rumors would give the Finnish national park an excuse to refuse permission in the future to anyone who wanted to cross Finland with dog sleds.

We later discovered that this man wielded a lot of power in the region (although he was not much liked) and that he owned one of the biggest reindeer herds in the country. So he was extremely wary of recent developments in local tourism – notably government-backed attempts to encourage winter activities such as cross-country skiing and snowmobile excursions.

We went straight across the lake, the dogs galloping joyfully, excited by the cold (–20°F; –30°C). The terrain was ideal, frozen to perfection. In France the dogs could never give their best. It had become difficult to find a route more than 20 miles long that didn't cross highways, fences or urban areas that broke the rhythm. Often the weather was too hot in a country where even the mountains were ill-suited to training sled dogs. The majority of mushers, after a few years of enthusiasm, would lose heart and give up. You can soon tire of keeping seven or eight dogs ready for snow that always comes too late, and then leading them around courses that they have covered a hundred times before. Dog sleds are best suited to the great open spaces – taiga, tundra and pack ice – and you have to find the means of getting there.

I'm tired of people who say how lucky I am to be able to take my dogs to such distant places, because luck has nothing to do with it. It's passion combined with sheer obstinacy that brought us this time to the high plateaus of Lapland, and on other occasions to the Carpathians or the pack ice off Labrador, or across Alaska and through the Rockies and even back to Siberia.

This small expedition to Finland and the Kola Peninsula was for one specific purpose only – that of preparing the dogs and testing out the equipment for a year-long expedition that I was planning with Diane and our young daughter. Montaine was growing – at only 18 months of age she was to become the most northerly of all French girls. With her parents she would live the life of a forest adventurer in the Rocky Mountains and the northern wastes of Canada.

The present expedition only confirmed what Jérôme and I had already predicted, that our sled teams would achieve the high performances we had hoped for. Crossing a laika with a Greenlander had given us dogs whose essential qualities were energy, speed and endurance. They admittedly had their faults too – notably an annoying tendency to spend the whole journey sniffing for the slightest whiff of potential game, even to the extent of following it if the trail was still fresh. Equally problematic was their quarrelsome temperament, which might easily lead to mutiny in the ranks.

Even with 450 pounds of baggage we made fast progress. Otchum led his elite team in great style, encouraging them farther each day from his position at the head of the line. We had our own special commands:

"Gee!" meant "go right."

"Yap!" meant "go left."

"Yap on" or "gee on" meant "carry on turning."

"Gee around" or "yap around" meant "do a U-turn on the spot" – a difficult maneuver for a long sled team to execute without becoming tied up in knots.

▲ Above:
*Returning to camp
after hunting for
capercaillie.*

▲ Top: *The
aurora borealis
creates a light
display above
our tent.*

▲ Above: *The
same tent that
was used in Jack
London's time.*

We plunged deep into the Russian taiga, crossing from one lake to the next through forests and open land, following the recent snowmobile tracks left by local trappers.

The team were continually sniffing at the scents of elk (moose), hare and capercaillie that had crossed our track. The whole region was overrun with game and the predators on their trail – sable, wolverine and wolves.

We allowed ourselves a few rest days, which we spent hunting and fishing. Fishing required a lot of physical effort, since before we could even start we had to dig a hole through a meter of ice. Our hunting endeavors were concentrated on capercaillie. We walked for several hours in snowshoes through seven-foot-deep snow before we finally caught a glimpse of one, surveying the forest from a vantage point at the top of a tall pine. The capercaillie has incredibly sharp senses – the slightest noise or movement and the bird will beat a noisy retreat. However, we eventually managed to kill one, which was immediately plucked, gutted, cooked and eaten with an appetite that was all the greater for the long hours of walking.

The dogs, meanwhile, were resting.

On our return journey, our team broke all records by covering some 60 miles in barely seven hours. We were clearly ready for the great adventure.

A SPECIAL DIET FOR SLED DOGS PREPARED BY THE RESEARCH STAFF OF PEDIGREE PAL FOR THE VANIER FAMILY EXPEDITION

A sled dog requires a perfectly balanced, digestible, energy- and nutrient-rich diet for optimum cold-resistance (e.g. at −40°F/−40°C) and the best sporting performance in terms of endurance and muscular power. A highly concentrated, energy-rich diet to fulfill all these requirements without overburdening the digestive tract was developed in the form of croquettes with the following composition: 34 percent protein, 29 percent fat, 27 percent carbohydrate; they provided a source of metabolizable energy at the rate of 460 kcal per gram.

If under normal conditions a dog weighing 65 lb (30 kg) requires approximately 1400 kcal per day, one can estimate that a sled dog of the same weight requires two-and-a-half times that amount, i.e. 3500 kcal per day.

Particular attention was paid to the choice of ingredients. Seven fat sources were used on the basis of nutritional value and the balance of essential fatty acids (linoleic and linolenic). They included chicken fat, fish oil, cocoa fat, soybean oil, pork fat and sunflower oil.

Eight protein sources were similarly chosen for their high nutritional value. These sources included chicken meat, fish, milk, eggs and vegetable proteins.

In the case of carbohydrates, rice and Indian corn were chosen as the main sources because they are easily digestible.

The diet was carefully formulated for the dogs' vitamin and mineral requirements: high levels of calcium, magnesium, iron and copper, and double or treble the normal amount of vitamins (but with only a slight increase in vitamin C).

The food was produced in croquette form by an extrusion process equivalent to continuous pressure-cooking to gelatinize the starches, at a moderate temperature to prevent any decomposition of the proteins that might reduce their nutritional value.

The product thus created was systematically monitored in the laboratory, and submitted to over fifty analytic tests for vitamins, amino-acids, minerals, trace elements, oxidation, cooking rates etc.

The final result was an extremely nutritional food adapted to the specific requirements of sled dogs.

OLIVIER CAPET

Riding through the Rockies

My first idea had been for us to take the whole pack of dogs, with the best of them carrying loads. It was a procedure that had once proved extremely effective on a hunting expedition with the Sekani Indians in the Rocky Mountains. It would enable the horses we would use to go much faster while at the same time training the dogs to carry a load – a skill that might come in very useful for other expeditions. A well-built sled dog should be capable of carrying a load of 45 pounds (20 kilos) for 20 miles without any difficulty.

This solution quickly proved impracticable, however, because we set off in the summer, when the presence of so much game was too much of a risk in view of our dogs' passion for hunting. Taking them with us through the game-filled valleys of the Rockies would be very dangerous for the new generation of fawns and other wild animals.

Charlie Boya, the chief of the Sekani Native American reserve, strongly advised us against it: "You shouldn't take them with you until the autumn when you arrive at the lake."

This was in fact the wisest solution. If the pack had been let loose in the great forests of British Columbia they would have created havoc, not to mention the risk that some of them might be killed if they went too close to bears in a ravine or a fast-flowing river.

The dogs would rejoin us on the shores of the lake where we had decided to build our cabin. This lake was about 150 miles from the nearest civilization as the crow flies, or 250–300 miles through the mountains – this was the distance from the road where Roy, the rancher who had sold us the four horses, set down the team with two hundredweight (100 kilos) of equipment and food.

◄ Opposite: *We were setting off on an expedition that was different from the others, with a little girl of 18 months – and Otchum of course.*

◄ Pages 104–5: *In Lapland, when Otchum crossed the border into Russia (the Kola Peninsula) he was effectively returning to his home country.*

THE INUIT

In their own language the word *inuit* means "people." The better-known term Eskimo is in fact a corruption of a Native American expression picked up by the first explorers, which means "eaters of raw meat." A pejorative term coined by hostile Native Americans was unlikely to be very popular with the Inuit themselves, who call their own language *inuktituk*.

THE NATIVE AMERICANS

There are two main groups of Native Americans in northern Canada: the Algonkians and the Athapaskans.

The Athapaskan group are mainly from north-west Canada and include the Kaska, Kutchin, Sekani, Slave, Tahltan, Chipewyan, Yellow-knife, Beaver and Carrier tribes.

The Algonkian Indians of northeastern Canada include the Montagnais, Cree and Naskapi, among others.

The team consisted of my wife Diane, our 18-month-old daughter Montaine, Otchum and myself.

We took him with us firstly for sentimental reasons, and secondly but more importantly on practical grounds. As an alarm dog, Otchum would provide our most effective protection against what we feared the most – the grizzlies, which were very common in this isolated corner of the Rockies.

For fifteen years I had traveled through countries where there were bears, but I'd never worried about them, because we'd always been careful to keep our distance while respecting certain basic rules. But I knew from various witnesses – trappers, Native Americans and other forest dwellers who crossed my path – that an incident with a grizzly bear was always possible. With a small girl in the party I was all the more on my guard, and Otchum even more so than me. Not a single grizzly could possibly approach without him giving us ample warning. One person warned is better prepared than two people suddenly faced with a bear as dangerous as the grizzly.

Witness all those people who are killed every year by this great beast, which is an indiscriminate fighter. A well-placed blow and your head will be sent hurtling up to 70 feet like a ping pong ball.

"I feel safe with him" said Diane, despite the fact that she was more apprehensive about meeting a bear than anything else.

For the moment, Montaine would continue to prattle from the safety of her mother's backpack, or comfortably installed in the two-seater saddle which we had had specially made for her for the journey.

She would smile at the black bears (not dangerous) which we often met as we crossed mountain pastures covered with flowers.

Otchum ran ahead of our little procession of four horses – two of them saddled and the other two loaded with equipment.

▲ Time for a siesta – Otchum watches over Montaine.

Despite the rain that accompanied the beginning of our trek (it rained on three days out of four), the landscape lost none of its grandeur. I loved riding through such wild, remote valleys with my wife and a little girl who was waking up to the world. There was a tremendous feeling of freedom. It was such a relief after a whole year of tension and anxiety while preparing for this year-long adventure.

We made gentle progress, following the tracks left by wild animals such as caribou and moose, towards Lake Thukada, which I had seen ten years before during the course of an eighteen-month expedition across the Rocky Mountains from south to north.

I had been so overwhelmed by the exceptional beauty of this high mountain lake, nestling in the very heart of the Rocky Mountains, that I had vowed to return there one day to realize my childhood dream of building my own log cabin.

Now at last I was to fulfill my dream. And even better, I was to do so with the assistance of my wife Diane, Montaine and, of course, Otchum.

Alas, the journey was to prove difficult. The rivers had become swollen with all the rain, so that we were often compelled to risk dangerous crossings or make long detours. There wasn't enough food. We came upon a grizzly by surprise and the horses bolted, carrying our rifles off with them, but the bear fortunately didn't attack. The mosquitoes, on the other hand, attacked with a vengeance as we trudged for miles across swamps and mountainsides. But nothing could dampen our immense joy at being there, all four of us together, on this amazing adventure.

Montaine adapted surprisingly well to her new conditions. She was full of the joys of life, passing the time playing with Otchum, who responded meekly to her every demand. Our long days of traveling were punctuated by her little piercing cries of "Tchou," which reduced us to fits of laughter.

In the evening, after Otchum had run a good 60 miles (four or five times the distance we had covered), he had only one wish – simply to rest at the foot of a bushy fir tree. But Montaine never gave him any peace. She would find his hiding place and climb delightedly onto his back, crying "A dada, dada." She would try to trap his tail when it moved, inspect his ears and pull his whiskers, and wedge pine cones, stones and various bits of food between his teeth.

It was moving to watch the little girl playing with this enormous dog, who could have knocked her over with just a shrug of his shoulder, yet who handled her with a gentleness that belied his wolf-like appearance. He was like a real big brother to her and we had total confidence in him. As long as Montaine stayed by him, we knew nothing could happen to her.

However, their newfound alliance created problems for us at mealtimes. Montaine soon discovered that Otchum was interested in everything we ate, and he quickly grasped that she was ready to give him anything, including the tastiest part of the meal. We forbade Montaine to share her meal with him, and told him off if he so much as came near her, with his customary nonchalant air. The games they played to divert our attention were an entertainment in themselves. We once caught Montaine with food stuffed in her little pockets, which she was carefully guarding to give it to her friend later in secret. Otchum's eyes would follow his little mistress's every deed and gesture, graciously obeying when she ordered him to sit. She used the one command she knew at every opportunity: "Tchou, sit!"

Otchum would obey her with a quick glance in my direction.

So there were three of us in love with this dog, who willingly loved us in return. Even the horses condescended to let Otchum be with them. He, on the other hand, appeared to think differently.

"These common herbivores are just about good enough for carrying things."

Otchum was allowed to frolic around their hoofs without them kicking him. But we never took this risk with Montaine. You simply couldn't trust a horse as much as you could trust a dog.

Otchum also spent many hours hunting, or rather chasing, moose, elk (wapiti) or wild sheep without posing much danger to the fawns or lambs. He was never short of food. We fished every day for trout to feed him, and he was a good hunter of small game, catching a partridge, a squirrel or a hare every day, not to mention eating the remains of our meals, which Montaine took great pleasure in giving him a mouthful at a time so as to prolong the pleasure.

Our arrival at the magnificent Lake Thukada, after several weeks of wandering, was a moving experience. It was indeed a magical moment.

THE ROCKY MOUNTAINS

"Mountains are to the rest of the earth what a violent muscular effort is to the body of man." (John Ruskin)

The Rockies are part of a vast mountain chain that extends the entire length of two continents, from Alaska to the Strait of Magellan. If you want to travel from the Atlantic to the Pacific Ocean, whether in North or in South America, you will need to cross this mountain chain at some point. The immense divide begins north of the Arctic Circle with the Brooks Range of northern Alaska. No one knows the exact length of the divide as it runs through Canada, the United States and Mexico, dwindles almost to sea level in Panama, and then rises again to form the Andes before finally reaching the southernmost point of South America. If you count all the twists and turns, it could be said to measure some 25,000 miles (more than 40,000 km) in length, which is a little more than the Earth's circumference.

▲ *Otchum and Montaine were the best of friends from the start.*

◄ *The cabin was finished just before the first snows.*

◄ Left: *To build the walls, we needed fifty 20-foot logs of stripped pine with a diameter of 10 inches. It took twelve to fifteen hours a day for six weeks to build the cabin of our dreams.*

OTCHUM

115

The snow-covered peaks, with their shining glaciers, were reflected in the blue waters of the lake, which trapped the silvery light only to return it to the verdant lower slopes striped with brown and gray patches of rock. Our eyes became lost in mountain pastures clothed in dark-green velvet, which contrasted with the deep blue of the sky, where a majestic eagle soared gracefully in precise circles.

This place was even more like a fairy tale than I remembered. Along the lake shore we found meadows covered with multicolored constellations of flowers, separating the forest of great pines from the transparent waters of the lake. At this point we stopped to enjoy the spectacle. The horses went on down to the water to drink and bathe limbs covered with horsefly and mosquito bites.

Otchum sniffed along the shoreline, where lots of beavers came to cut down trees (mainly alders and a few willows) and also to wash themselves – one of the favorite pastimes of these little flat-tailed lumberjacks.

Now it was time to build our cabin.

I felled the trees and cut the trunks to size.

Diane removed the bark and filled the cracks with moss.

Montaine played and Otchum watched.

Three horses rested. The fourth, broken in for the task, pulled the trees, some weighing more than four hundredweight (200 kilos), along the lake shore.

We worked long hours but found immense pleasure in building such a fine log cabin in this beautiful place.

Otchum and Montaine would slip away to spend the day exploring the area around the camp. For Diane and me, who kept alternate watch, it became increasingly difficult to keep an eye on them. If we weren't careful, Montaine might walk miles away from the camp on Otchum's trail. We soon realized there was only one effective way of calling her back, and that was by calling Otchum. She would reappear some time after the dog, out of breath and calling "Tchou, tchou!"

Otchum would gently wag his tail as he allowed her to kiss his nose. What a pair!

The cabin was finished by the time of the first snow. We were really proud of it. And it certainly looked grand, gold-tinted in the evening sunlight between the blue of the lake and the deep green of the forest as it vied with the immaculate white of the permanent snows above.

▲ *Montaine became inseparable from her playmate.*

▲ Above: *A Canada goose.*

▶ Right: *Diane was greatly attached to Otchum, whom she had first met in Siberia.*

The pack

The sound of an engine in the sky reminded us that our cabin might be two months on foot from the nearest civilization, but it was only three hours in a modern seaplane. Inside the seaplane were ten dogs, the sled, window panes for the cabin, a few tools, some food, and in charge of all this Jérôme and Alain, who were also going to take our horses back to Prince George.

Montaine, who had nearly forgotten that other people existed, simply couldn't get over the shock of the arrival. She was overcome with amazement at the sight of a howling pack of ten overexcited dogs jumping straight from the seaplane into the water.

Otchum was similarly overcome, but not exactly delighted to see his sons. He had got used to being without them and wasn't very happy to share with ten other dogs the life of luxury he'd enjoyed for five months. With a bite here and a growl there, Otchum defended what he considered to be his own territory – the cabin and its immediate surroundings. The dogs seemed almost glad to be driven away: they had no wish to confront him, as it would only be a waste of time. They preferred to explore the neighborhood, sniffing at the trails of unfamiliar animals such as moose, beaver and bear, or to bathe in the lake or bark from behind at the horses, who didn't enjoy the joke.

I had great difficulty recognizing Ouktu and Kurvik – two pups from Ska's most recent litter, who had been born a month before our departure. These two magnificent seven-month specimens had almost reached their adult stature despite a general air of ungainliness. The dogs were all in tiptop condition, with magnificent fur and strong muscles – true athletes who wanted nothing more than to launch themselves across the snow. That wouldn't be long now. The thermometer was plummeting, and the snow on the mountains was invading the green pastures on the slopes.

◄ Opposite: *The pack, now complete, was assembled beneath the shade of the pine forest behind our cabin.*

We settled the dogs under the pines by the shore. The main chain was drawn tight in a sinuous pattern among the trees. The dogs were all attached to this by individual chains that gave them a certain amount of freedom without allowing them too near their neighbors.

We always allowed two or three dogs to run free, but only in turns, because they would run off and hunt miles away from the camp and we wouldn't see them again until the evening. Even when we let them loose in twos or threes, we had to avoid certain combinations such as Amarok and Baikal, or Nanook and Voulk. As a general rule it was better to mix dogs from different litters. Ouktu and Kurvik were given free rein nearly all the time, because they were young dogs and I wanted them to run around and develop their muscles. Otchum remained free both day and night, but we occasionally tied him up near the rest of the pack, partly to get him used to the chain again, and partly so that he could reintegrate himself with the pack despite his preference for living in luxury with us.

The first time we did this, Otchum really made us laugh. He was miserable and furious at the same time, his tail drooping, his fur bristling and his eyes flashing. He looked as if he might burst into tears: "Me, Otchum, on a chain!"

Otchum clearly needed to come down from his pedestal and to relearn some of the basic principles of living with a pack of sled dogs. To make this work we adopted a graduated approach: ten minutes on the first day, an hour on the second, and a whole night a few days later. It was worrying for us to notice a change in his attitude towards the other dogs in the pack. He was no longer one of them, even though he remained the uncontested leader after one or two quarrels with Baikal, who had been toying with the idea of taking over.

We hoped things would return to normal after a period of mutual adaptation, because the team had to be well integrated in order to function properly. If Otchum no longer behaved towards the others in the same way that he had done previously, the others would respond differently too. There was the pack and then there was Otchum, and this affected my reply when

people asked me how many dogs were in my team: "Ten dogs and Otchum." He was so different from the others despite the fact that he was their father.

▲ *The lake was home to trout weighing more than 20 pounds.*

Ska, their mother, was in good health even though, like so many mothers in this world, she had suffered a bit from successive pregnancies. But I doubted she would able to keep up for very long with the rhythm set by the young dogs in the team, especially since I was planning to train them to maintain a fast pace over a long period. By now Ska had earned a peaceful retirement. She was a rascal, but I was very fond of her.

During the month of September, the wild animals from the valleys and mountains around us became more and more visible as they fled the onset of winter. The bears were gorging on blueberries, while the geese were gathering along the lake shore, sheltering in bays protected from the wind. At night the moose were engaged in mighty combats that resounded across the taiga. The wolves were gathering in packs and trying out their voices. The goats and sheep were returning to the rocks and pastures, while herds of caribou were beginning their long migration across the mountains.

The mountains and everything that lived there seemed to tremble like a forest before a storm. We could sense that something big was on the way – winter.

The dogs were excited too, prancing about and howling as a pack more and more often. Their voices seemed to blend with all the others that resounded across the taiga as if summoning the cold. The lakes and rivers would soon be frozen over enough so that we could begin our long travels.

The only animal we were not glad to see was a large grizzly that took to prowling around our cabin in the middle of the night. His visits continued for a week and we became increasingly worried. This bear was afraid of nothing. It approached within a few yards of our door, ransacked everything it found, and circled around the dogs as they barked furiously and pulled on their chains. If the grizzly came closer there would be carnage. A punch here and a punch there, and by early morning there would be nothing left of our dogs. The only one we released was Otchum, who, being experienced, always kept a safe distance between himself and the bear – just enough to give him time to retreat if it charged. But he refused to let it out of his sight, and his barks gave us an idea of its whereabouts.

For some five or six hours, from eleven o'clock to four in the morning, Otchum kept on harassing the bear, following it and barking furiously whenever it moved. I presume the bear must have got used to his antics. We had hung everything we could out of its reach, but all that happened was that the "repair bill" become higher every night, not to mention the growing risk that an "accident" might befall our dogs if not ourselves. The bear was afraid of nothing. We had tried everything, even setting off flares, but the bear just made fun of us. We had to kill it, much as we disliked this radical solution. Bears can't be eaten, and we weren't used to killing an animal for any other reason than satisfying our physical hunger. But we were left with no choice.

There was still a problem because the bear always appeared at night, when it was not visible enough for me to be sure of killing it with a single bullet, which was absolutely essential in order to prevent it from charging at me. Shooting it in the middle of the night might be tantamount to turning the gun on myself – a kind of suicide.

"How are we going to get rid of it, then?" asked Diane at the end of her rope. We could no longer sleep at night and the prowler even seemed to haunt us during the day.

Then on the evening of the seventh day, the sky, which for a week had been overcast, suddenly cleared and the sun shed its rosy glow over the jagged peaks of the mountains. Perhaps the change in the weather affected the bear's behavior, but for once it arrived in the evening before nightfall.

Despite being extremely anxious, I remained resolute as I silently approached the bear, ready with a bullet in the barrel of my rifle. Having left my Winchester (a repeating rifle) with Jérôme and Alain on their return to Prince George, I was armed with only a single bullet in my rifle.

So there was no question of misfiring the first time. It had to be a good shot – if not it would be my last. There would be no time to see if the bear was wounded and about to charge me, for there was a 99-percent chance that it would do so under the circumstances.

My heart was beating fast but I didn't tremble. All the dogs were tied up, including Otchum, who would have distracted the bear while I approached. I was soon close to the beast, which after a short turn in the forest was coming straight towards me. It forded the river and lumbered in the direction of the cabin. I was exactly in its path. It was coming closer – 100 yards, 80 yards, 50 yards ...

I shot, and the bullet hit the grizzly square in the chest. The bear growled horribly and, rearing up on its hind legs, swiped the air with its enormous paws as if trying to tear an imaginary enemy to pieces.

I hurriedly opened up my rifle to remove the spent bullet, trying not to give in to the panic that came over me as I became aware that the bear had seen me.

▶ Opposite: *The hierarchy in a pack can be established by mutual consent, but it generally happens after one dog has imposed certain conditions on another by force.*

▶ Pages 128–9: *The notorious grizzly bear had posed such a danger to us and the dogs that we had been forced to kill it.*

"Quick, quick!" I said to myself. I could see a terrible hatred in its eyes as they fixed on me for a tenth of a second.

The wounded grizzly fell back on its front paws and launched itself in my direction, its mouth open and its eyes tinged with red. A few more yards and it would be on top of me before I had time to reload my rifle.

"I'm done for!" I thought.

At that moment, in the corner of my eye I noticed a black shape suddenly darting into view from the left between me and the bear. The bear, interrupted in mid-charge by this unexpected visitor, turned to attack my rescuer, who was none other than Otchum.

This gave me just enough time to reload my rifle, get the neck of the bear in my sights, and shoot it as it charged my bravely defiant dog.

The bear collapsed, and that was the end.

I walked silently towards Otchum, my eyes full of tears of recognition and love.

"Otchum, my Otchum, how on earth did you get loose? How did you know I needed you?"

At the margins of our sensory perceptions there begins a world that most of us are totally unaware of. When mankind finally admits that animals possess faculties that often defy comprehension, then we will acknowledge a difference that may help us to come down from our pedestal.

In the depths of winter

"In Siberia the winter lasts twelve months and the rest is summer."

"In Canada there are four seasons: July, August, September and winter!"

(sayings about winter)

The temperature was –20°F (–30°C). One part of the lake with deep water and a peppering of islands was the first area to retain the ice despite the wind. As the snow had not yet covered the land, the lake was the only place where we could use the sled. The dogs were pawing the ground with as much impatience as we felt. This reminded me of an occasion in Siberia when we were waiting on our little island at the northern end of the great Lake Baikal for the cold to freeze the lake. One morning we had set off with our thirty dogs across a two-inch layer of blue ice that was so transparent that we could see the fish swimming beneath it.

We were just as impatient as then, but just as cautious as well. The ice wasn't thick yet, and although there were some sections that would carry us, there were others where the surface would crack as soon we approached. Before leading the dogs onto the ice, I went out on foot to decide on the area to which our activity was to be restricted. The section where we could venture in total safety was not very large, but it was all we could expect to start with. Otchum came with me, and like me he seemed to be testing the frozen surface as if he knew what was going on.

The previous evening, when I had unpacked the harnesses from their enormous canvas bag, I could see the sparks of recognition in Otchum's eyes. That morning, I was certain, he knew we would return to the ice with the sled.

◄ Opposite: *Having a drink at –40°F (–40°C) during a break in the middle of the day.*

OTCHUM

131

ORGANIZING A SLED TEAM

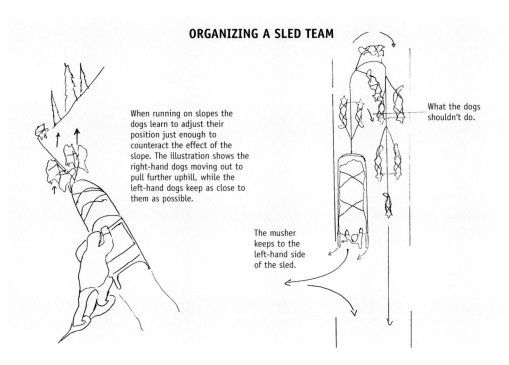

When running on slopes the dogs learn to adjust their position just enough to counteract the effect of the slope. The illustration shows the right-hand dogs moving out to pull further uphill, while the left-hand dogs keep as close to them as possible.

What the dogs shouldn't do.

The musher keeps to the left-hand side of the sled.

At first I harnessed only five of the dogs. Otchum took the lead, of course. Torok was the strongest and the best of my wheel dogs, so he joined Baikal just in front of the sled. I put Amarok and Ska in the second row.

"Sit!"

The five dogs obeyed, but kept on prodding the snow with their front paws, creating small lumps against which they braced themselves ready for my next command.

The sled shot sharply forward with the reins taut. Montaine witnessed the spectacle, her eyes almost popping out of her head in amazement.

I made several turns around the ice at a good gallop, covering about four or five times the length of a football field. I then returned to find Diane and Montaine. I added two more dogs to the team: Nanook and Voulk, who were brothers from the same litter.

Montaine clapped her hands as we set off. Could she possibly imagine that one day she would travel like this with her best friend in harness?

"Go, Tchoum, go!"

She kept on cheering us on and clapping her hands, refusing to return to the cabin until she had seen us complete at least fifty circuits.

From now on the intensive training began. Every day the cold and the snow extended our territory. Soon the whole lake was frozen, giving us access to all the valleys whose waters flowed into it. Before long everything was covered with snow and we could go everywhere, as far as we wanted. It was the beginning of a wonderful period for the dogs, and one of my most enjoyable times on the ice. From sunrise to sunset we explored this vast region along the tracks that we made through the snow, with no boundaries apart from the horizon. We often went as a family, with Diane and myself on the runners and Montaine just in front of us at the back of the sled, bundled up in thick furs to protect her from the cold. We swept gracefully along the frozen rivers that provided the best routes.

At this pace the young dogs made fast progress, while Otchum became a better lead dog than ever. The three youngest dogs – Oukiok at fifteen months, and Ouktu and Kurvik at just eight months – had been harnessed for the first time at Lake Thukada. But by this time they were pulling like their brothers. The adults that formed the rest of the team had become true athletes, obeying the smallest of my commands with the utmost precision.

It was a real pleasure to execute difficult maneuvers such as a U-turn, in which all eleven dogs seemed almost to roll over on top of one other in order to return alongside the sled and continue in the opposite direction without becoming entangled. Such a feat demanded a lot of experience and skill on the part of the dogs, who each had to wait until exactly the right moment before turning. It needed only one of the eleven dogs to turn too early to reduce the whole pack to a tangled heap. The lead dog plays a vital role in the execution of such a maneuver. As he retraces his steps alongside the rest of the team, he stops any impatient dog from turning until his rein has become loose – all that's required for this is a brief growl or a snap of the jaws. A

▶ Pages 134–5: *Pushing, pulling and straightening up are the main tasks for the person at the back.*

MAKING MOCCASINS

Knot

Foot

Heel

Moccasin viewed from behind

Viewed from the side

Knot

Third piece

Second piece

Order of sowing

5

3

4

1

2

U-turn with my eleven dogs soon became the showpiece of our sled team.

We trained for what seemed like ages to perfect a whole series of delicate maneuvers, including oblique descents, crossing partly frozen rivers, and 45-degree turns. The last of these required the dogs first to go straight on, upon which half the team had to retrace their steps and then carry on to the left or right – a technique used to stop the sled from becoming jammed. The team was learning how to deal with every kind of situation they could possibly be faced with over hundreds of miles across a whole variety of terrain, including mountains, forests, rivers, lakes, high plateaus and tundra.

Every morning we set off at sunrise to complete a tour of all the traps that we had placed along a ten-mile track. Every snare or trap along the track was designed to catch a fur animal (for making moccasins for us or fur clothing for Montaine), and each of them was marked out with a piece of red ribbon tied around a tree. The dogs learned to recognize these markers and would stop of their own accord when they reached a trap. I didn't even need to tie them or plant an anchor in the snow to stop them going off without me. They waited obediently, and if it occurred to any of them to leave (Oumiak, Kurvik or Amarok), Otchum would prevent them and punish them sharply to stop them trying the same thing again. I taught them to set off without me if, for example, I should be in front of them making a track or releasing a trap. One whistle and the team would take off towards me. Then I would either catch the sled on the move or make the dogs stop on command when they caught up with me.

We functioned perfectly together, sharing in the same joy at the freedom of long excursions across the vast frozen expanses.

The whole team had got to know Montaine, who by now was well acquainted with all of them. Her favorites were Ska and Ouktu, who was so like Otchum that she called him "Little Tchou." When we traveled with her on the sled, she would delight in repeating the names of all the dogs:

"Great Torok."

"Trok!" she replied.

"Brave Nanook."

"Anook!"

"Baikal the fighter."

"Baka!"

"Voulk the wolf."

"Vouk!"

"Bravo! – Oukiok with the golden eyes."

"Kok!"

"Ska the mother."

"Ska!"

"Bravo again!"

And so it went on – and if the dogs turned around when she called their name, her happiness knew no bounds.

Having brought a camera with our baggage, we were able to take plenty of photos of our little "child of the snows" with the dogs. It was both moving and very rewarding to see our tiny daughter talking to this pack of large, wolf-like dogs. When she walked alongside the sled team, one or two of them would invariably give her face a lick under the guise of a kiss. Montaine would then laugh uproariously, her breath freezing immediately in the cold air so that her little face became surrounded with a frosty halo that shone in the sunlight. The camera purred as if to echo our enjoyment.

THE TALE OF THE GIRL WHO MARRIED A DOG

This is one of the oldest known legends of the northern peoples. It exists in several different versions, such as those of the Native Americans and the Inuit, not to mention the various Asiatic peoples. According to the Inuit, the girl was called Vinagumasuituk or "the girl who refused to marry." Her father finally married her off to a stranger, who then revealed himself to be a dog in disguise. Their children, according to the Inuit, were the ancestors of all human races. Some of them looked like people and these became the Inuit (the word means "people"). The others looked more like dogs and these were the "other" people.

Later on the father threw his daughter in the sea, but she resisted and held on to the boat. So her father cut off her fingers, which became whales, seals, walruses, narwhals etc.

The girl plunged into the depths of the sea and became a goddess.

ANIMALS IN THE SNOW

Animal experts, notably the Russian specialist Formozov, place animals in three categories on the basis of how they deal with deep snow:
- chionophobes, who hate deep snow
- chionophiles, who live within it
- chionophores, who deal with it moderately successfully.

It is the pressure exerted by an animal's foot, measured in grams per square centimeter (g/cm^2) or pounds per square inch (lb/sq in), which determines whether the foot sinks in deep snow or remains on the surface. It has been calculated that a foot exerting a pressure of less than 40 g/cm^2 (0.6 lb/sq in) will not sink into the snow.

Here are some animal examples:
- ptarmigan: 13 g/cm^2 (0.2 lb/sq in)
- fox: 28 g/cm^2 (0.4 lb/sq in)
- capercaillie: 50 g/cm^2 (0.7 lb/sq in)
- moose: 900 g/cm^2 (13 lb/sq in).

Nature has never stinted in providing special ways for animals to deal with the snow in the same way that we use snowshoes: feathers on a bird's foot, horny growths on an animal's toes, and the thick fur that grows on a hare's paws in the autumn.

► Right: *A ptarmigan.*

▼ Below: *The face of a Siberian reindeer.*

► Right: *An Arctic hare.*

► Opposite: *Too late – the ptarmigan has flown.*

OTCHUM

The great journey

When Montaine took up her position at the back of the sled, did she realize that in the heart of winter she would cross the whole northern section of the Rocky Mountains and then go on from the Yukon all the way into Alaska? Probably not, despite all the explanations we gave her.

Otchum, of course, knew we were off on a long expedition. He knew because the sled was heavily loaded, which meant several weeks of travel. He was not particularly bothered by this. Now that he had crossed the whole of Siberia and Lapland, northern Canada was no more than an extension of a single great snowbound adventure.

On this occasion, however, some of the equipment was special, as though my family and his were setting off like a boat crew facing a long and difficult crossing. The Rocky Mountains and the Yukon weren't noted for being kind to travelers. Jack London had provided us with more detail than anyone else about this country which "in its meanness seems to have disowned the land of men."

On the sled sat our most precious treasure, liberally swathed in furs. For traveling at –40°F (–40°C) I had adapted a heating system for her that had originally been developed for keeping a camera at a "reasonable" temperature. It consisted of a small charcoal briquette that burned slowly to give off a steady heat, and that was supplied with air by means of a small battery–driven ventilator. It was placed inside a thick quilted coat that was in turn wrapped in the furs, allowing sufficient heat through to keep our little girl comfortable despite outside temperatures of around –40°F (–40°C). Without this system we could not have traveled for more than one or two hours a day – and Alaska is a long way from Lake Thukada (well over 1000 miles).

Since the start of winter the dogs had already covered at least 2,000 miles altogether, and between 20 and 50 miles a day since the lake had frozen over. Needless to say, it was a group of

◄ Opposite: *One of us used to assist the dogs by going ahead of them in snowshoes to break up the snow.*

▲ Above: *At −50°F (−45°C) you expose as little as possible to the air.*

◀ Left: *The sled team crossing Lake Thukada.*

▲ Above: *We always kept some water in a thermos for when Montaine was thirsty en route. Even at two she could walk through deep snow.*

▶ Right: *Few people have used dog sleds to cross the Rockies in British Columbia, because the rivers don't freeze hard and are dangerous even when they do.*

Area: 2.5 million sq
miles or 7 million km^2 –
not far short of the
contiguous USA.
The Canadian North
extends for 3,000 miles
(5,000 km) between
the Pacific and the
Atlantic.
Population: less than 8
inhabitants per 100 sq
miles (5 per 100 km^2) –
300,000 in sub-arctic
regions, 30,000 in
arctic regions, only 500
in polar regions.

genuine athletes that lined up for departure on this expedition
we had dreamed of for such a long time, even if with a certain
amount of apprehension.

"Go, Otchum!"

"No, Tataine do it!"

Montaine, whose speech had developed surprisingly fast
during recent weeks, was claiming her right to direct the dogs
herself.

She already knew the main commands, although she didn't
give them at the most appropriate moments. Fortunately the
dogs could distinguish between her orders and mine. Otherwise
we might have taken off in completely the wrong direction, or
we might have stopped at any time and failed to start again at
the right moment.

With the sled carrying more than 6 cwt (300 kg), the team
performed extraordinarily well in the deep snow. Pulling a heavy
sled across a hard surface is not exactly an easy exercise, but
dragging it through a couple of feet of snow is positively heroic.
We helped them as much as we could by walking in front of
Otchum and leaving a track with large snowshoes that broke up
the snow, or with our feet if it wasn't very deep. The deeper the
track we made, the more it would help the dogs.

If the going was really too hard for them, we would lighten
the sled by removing the sacks of dog food, which weighed as
much as 4 cwt (200 kg) at the start of the journey. The
following evening, after the tent had been erected, I would
return to fetch the sacks along a track that by now would have
turned to ice. Diane and Montaine waited for me in the warmth
of the tent. Diane used the time to saw and split the wood
which I'd gathered in the neighboring woods before leaving – a
dead pine tree with nice gray timber that had been stripped of
its bark.

The dogs enjoyed galloping along with an empty sled on a
hard surface. What a change from the daytime, when the pack
had struggled through deep snow to pull a heavy load! We often
returned after dark, and I loved these nocturnal trips. I could
watch the northern lights as they rolled about the sky, and hear

a wolf pack howling in the distance like a wild chant performed by some ancient choir. I was totally in tune with the dogs. We had become like a single entity enclosed in a bubble, like a phantom vessel gliding silently through the immaculate whiteness of a lunar landscape.

With the dog sled the main enemy of progress was weight. Each dog required 28 oz (800 g) of dehydrated food per day, which amounted to nearly 22 lb (10 kg) for the whole pack. Just imagine what that would have come to on this trip, given that we would have to travel for forty days before the supply could be replenished. The total amount would have been some 8 cwt (400 kg) of food, plus an additional 2.5 cwt (120 kg) for the equipment (tent, stove, clothing, ax, saw etc.). The only solution was to find meat along the way, whether from moose or caribou. This would provide 7–9 lb (3–4 kg) of meat per dog, or about 1 cwt (50 kg) for the whole pack. But in general a whole day was required – sometimes longer – in order to hunt, kill and carve up a moose or caribou and bring it back to camp.

A caribou would provide meat for a maximum of two days, so if two days were needed for hunting the gain was nil. A moose provided four days' worth of meat, but on the other hand a day would have been lost hunting the beast, which could be fed to the dogs in the evening, while the rest of the meat had to be carried on the sled, adding a further 3 cwt (150 kilos) to the load. The result of this left very little margin for maneuver.

We couldn't hunt for the first two weeks anyway, because the sled was too heavy to cope with the additional weight of meat. Therefore it was best to hunt when the food supplies were running low and when the animals took less time to hunt. But you can't treat nature like a well–stocked shop, especially in

NAVIGATING IN THE FAR NORTH

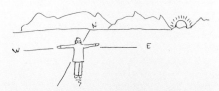

Some people claim to be able to navigate by examining moss or the thickness of the bark on the trees, or even from the effects of the prevailing winds, which produce certain indicators – but such people are not to be trusted.
The only infallible indicators are the Sun and the polestar. The Sun rises more or less in the east or northeast, so in clear weather it is easy to navigate.

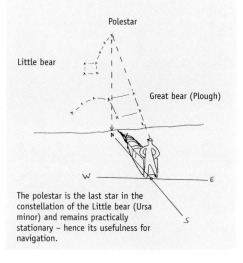

The polestar is the last star in the constellation of the Little bear (Ursa minor) and remains practically stationary – hence its usefulness for navigation.

▶ Pages 148–9: *For going fast the ideal temperatures are between –5°F (–20°C) and –30°F (–35°C).*

winter. Herd animals may desert one area completely in order to overwinter in another, which is where one would have to go in order to find them. And when an animal has been found, it still needs to be approached and killed in a place from which the meat can be carried away – always assuming that you've managed to shoot it successfully in the first place, which is by no means easy from a distance.

So, all in all, hunting for meat isn't as easy as ordering a joint from the butcher, quite apart from which some people find it much more cruel.

I have several times found myself in critical situations, but our knowledge of the forest and of the animals within it has always enabled us to get ourselves out of trouble before it was too late. On this occasion, too, we were compelled to trust in our good fortune, and arrived at our first relay station in extremis, with an empty sled and empty stomachs to boot.

The dogs were just as surprised as Montaine to see a car, a road, houses and people again.

"What's that, Daddy?"

"It's a car, which is a bit like a sled except it has wheels instead of dogs – and an engine too …"

"Oh!"

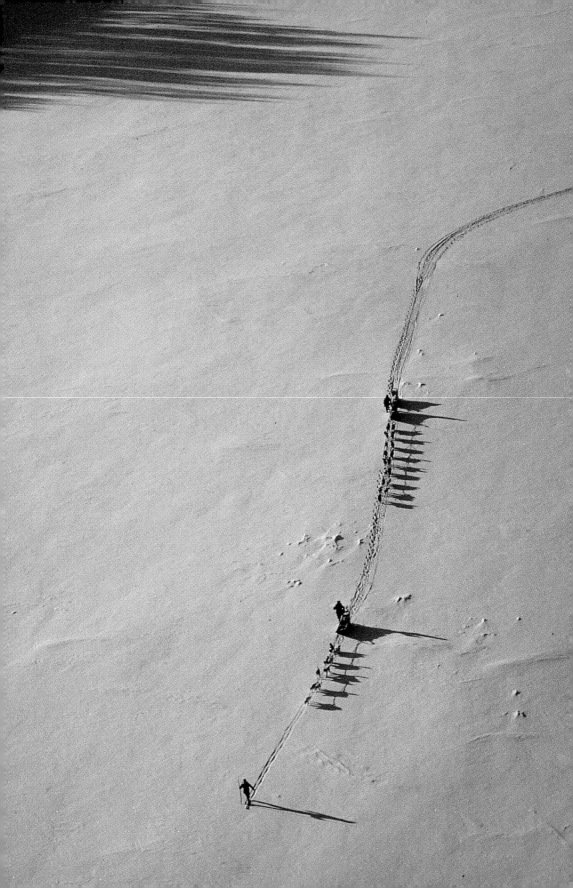

On the track of the Yukon Quest

The Yukon Quest is the toughest race in the world. This is on record. With a length of 1000 miles (1,600 km), it's not only the longest in the world together with the Iditarod, but more importantly it's the toughest race of all – with a capital T! Only professionals enter this race, having spent the whole year training up to 200 or 300 participating dogs, whose performances are measured and managed by computer.

The race takes ten days, with an average of one to three hours sleep in 24 hours. The average temperature overall is –40°F (–40°C), dropping at times to –65°F (–55°C). The course has become the stuff of legends. Men and dogs become heroes, and sometimes even legends in their own right. The race takes place in the coldest part of the winter across the Yukon and Alaska.

We arrived at Whitehorse a week after the race had started with the intention of using the track, this being the only link to Dawson. This ancient trail was once used by the gold seekers of the Klondike as a substitute for the River Yukon, which was known as Death River on account of its unstable winter ice – to use such a route would have been suicide.

The gold seekers carved a track across the Black Hills – a name given to the bare mountains of the Yukon and all these desert regions. They were a kind of "no man's land" separating Whitehorse and Dawson, because between these two villages there was nothing.

"You're mad!" they kept on saying in Whitehorse when we told them we were going to Dawson along the track of the Yukon Quest with a two-year old girl on the sled.

But we went nonetheless and the dogs made good time. Despite the heavy sled, we covered stages of up to 60 miles (nearly 100 km) in length every day.

That inevitably gave me an idea ...

◄ Opposite: *On the white surface of the ice there was nothing to distract the eye.*

Years ago, when I had followed the Yukon Quest for Ushuaïa Broadcasting in order to make a film about the race, my comment to my friend and companion Karl Gérin had been "Never!" We had seen these men almost exceed their physical capacity to arrive at a checkpoint after 24 hours of non-stop racing at –40°F (–40°C) through a horrific blizzard, only to continue at the dead of night just an hour later without even having slept. "Never!" I had said.

But there is a saying that goes "Never say never." Since then I had traveled with dogs for twelve years, and crossed tens of thousands of miles of taiga, tundra, mountains and ice. So I could honestly say that I didn't have a lot more to learn. I had exactly the right experience to enable me to travel for weeks at –40°F (–40°C) in complete safety with a little girl on the sled.

If I took part in a race like the Yukon Quest, I might learn a tremendous amount that would justify my participation – and, more importantly, it occurred to me that with the right training our team could spring a surprise on the others.

Nowadays all the professional mushers line up for the Yukon Quest with teams of Alaskans – the Formula One sled dog that is the product of careful cross-breeding with various races that were built for speed. These dogs no longer look much like sled dogs. They run with boots on their feet and coats on their backs simply because their fur isn't thick enough to stand a fierce blizzard at –60°F (–50°C). Nowadays even the mushers are beginning to question whether Alaskans can break records in a squall. The breeders have surely gone too far in their selection, their vision clouded by such factors as speed and endurance, to the detriment of certain qualities inherent in northern breeds that are vital to a race such as the Yukon Quest. Every year the teams are slowed down by a fierce blizzard or a sudden drop in temperature.

Now my dogs were quite capable of getting through a blizzard at –60°F (–50°C), and from then on they might be able to go almost as fast as the Formula Ones, or at least achieve the same overall time. A Frenchman in the Yukon Quest would be a real event (my name was already being heard in such circles).

THE GREAT SLED RACES

The **Iditarod**: 1,049 miles (1,688 km) across Alaska from Anchorage to Nome. Taking place at the beginning of March, this is one of the two longest races in the world, the other being the **Yukon Quest**. It's also the most famous. It has four times been won by a woman, Susan Butcher. Rick Swenson, known as "The King," has headed the race five times. Founded by Joe Redington, the race has produced higher averages than the Yukon Quest, but is less difficult on account of the number of stages, the easier route, and the assistance provided.

There are other big races in the USA and Canada: the **Lac Saint-Jean** race in Quebec Province, the **Kobuk** north of the Arctic Circle, and the **Beargrease Sled Dog Marathon** in Minnesota.

In Europe, the **Alpirod** once enjoyed an excellent reputation as far away as Alaska on account of the excellent logistics and rigorous preparation of the course. Unfortunately it was discontinued through lack of sponsorship, and the last event was in 1995. Founded in 1988, the race took place during the third and fourth weeks of January over a 500-mile course that went through France, Switzerland, Italy and Austria.

Sprint races involve small teams of three or six dogs, or sometimes more, depending on how much power is required. They take place over very short distances of 3–6 miles.

A Frenchman with a unique team like mine would attract even more interest. And if after a few days we were rivaling the best of them, we would be laughing!

I had made my decision. It wouldn't be the following year, because I would have to make careful preparations, but after two years I would be there at the start.

After all, one thing that was still missing from Otchum's list of achievements was a place in one of the great sled races.

The nearer we came to Dawson and the end of our great journey, the more I talked to Diane about this exciting project. I was surprised to find myself noting points on the map where we could find water or dead wood along the track. In two years' time such information might come in useful …

▲ Above: *In a blizzard at −75°F (−60°C) − the kind of situation that makes this race so exciting.*

▲ Top: *The start of the toughest of all the sled-dog races.*

▶ Right: *There are eight checkpoints dispersed at intervals along the thousand-mile route. These are where veterinary surgeons check out the dogs, taking some of them out of the race.*

Dawson

It was somehow symbolic when on our arrival in the legendary town we passed Jack London's cabin. Here was the birthplace of stories such as *Call of the Wild* – stories that fired the dreams of my youth and that were perhaps the reason for my being there now.

Diane and I were happy and proud of what we had achieved during the year in which Montaine had awoken to such a beautiful and simple world. She was talking now, repeating words such as "dogs," "sled," "ice" and "moose." Now she would have to learn some more words: "car," "house," "television", "school." At all events she was in radiant health. She laughed all day and her smiles were full of sunshine.

The dogs were in peak form and would have been able to return by the same route they had come. But spring had arrived, and after a year away we would have to return home.

Before leaving Dawson, I was keen to make one more sled trip with my eleven dogs – a run to the Alaskan border and back, which meant 50 miles along the frozen River Yukon.

I had traveled along this same river a few years before, but in high summer and by a form of transport that was just as natural as a dog sled: a raft that we had built just downstream from Dawson, and on which we had traveled 750 miles downstream. We had then carried on upstream by canoe to the divide that separates the Yukon and Kuskokwim watersheds. It had been a difficult journey. But after five months of traveling we had finally reached the salt waters of the Bering Strait. On the opposite side was Siberia. That was where the project had been born to cross the legendary wastes of Siberia. At that time Otchum had not even been conceived in his mother's womb.

The years had passed and more stories had been written. I was pleased to be able to write about a high-performance sled team as original as this one, trotting gently for hours on end towards Alaska at 10 mph without ever slowing down.

◄ Opposite: *Dawson, the legendary town of the famous Klondike gold rush. The walls of its wooden buildings often have scenes painted on them.*

▶ Opposite: *Jérôme and the dogs take an early morning run through the forests of the Jura.*

▶ Pages 162–3: *The race is a solitary struggle. Alone with his dogs, the musher who wins is the one who makes the fewest mistakes.*

The following day we would return by truck to Vancouver, then by airplane to Paris.

That summer the dogs would enjoy a well-earned rest, running freely around a park specially created for them in a quiet corner of the High Jura. To keep them in condition we would buy a four-wheel drive vehicle for them to pull along the forest paths in the early morning.

In September they would return to the north, which was the only place for training a pack of sled dogs to a high enough performance level for a long-distance race.

My hope was that Air Canada would assist by providing airplane tickets in exchange for publicity space, and that Pedigree Pal would continue to collaborate with us too.

It's good to have a head full of dreams, although the chance to realize them may depend on the color of your money. But nothing but blizzards could stop anybody who really wanted to participate in one of the biggest dog-sled races in the world.

Northern Quebec

Everything worked out OK with Pedigree Pal and Air Canada. So Jérôme and I had found the best possible strategy for entering a competitive team in the Yukon Quest, by spending a whole winter training our dogs in northern Quebec. The last place on the map was the village of Gérardville. North of here there was nothing but thousands of miles of ice and snow, which made it the ideal place for training. Every day the dogs ran between 25 and 60 miles across this white wilderness.

At the same time the full-length film of our expedition through the Rockies, *Child of the Snows*, hit the movie screens and was rapturously received by the critics. This meant that soon I might finally be able to fulfill my long-held dream of making a film adaptation of a novel I had written about the far north (*Solitudes blanches*, Actes Sud, 1992). I wanted it to be a film about what the north really is like, with real-life cold, real-life ice and real-life blizzards. This film would be a first. We would travel for a month through Inuit territory at temperatures of –40°F (–40°C). No tricks – it would be the real thing.

We would need two sled teams, Jérôme's and mine. The film would be a paean to the far north, showing some of its most beautiful landscapes in the mountains, the taiga, the tundra and on the ice.

Otchum was going to be a film star.

The story was going to be about a race between two old friends, two trappers and a woman who was half Native American.

It would show genuine caribou hunts, polar bears ambling across the ice, wolf attacks beneath the northern lights, and musk-oxen charging through impressive gorges. Into this film event we were going to invest our fifteen years of experience, skill, and knowledge.

Meanwhile the dogs would run, achieving amazing performances such as 200 miles in 20 hours. We would be in the front team.

▲ Above: *The whole team – a real family photo.*

▶ Right: *Amarok (behind) and Nanook (in front).*

Epilogue

Stories always come to an end, and this one has a tragic ending. I won't beat around the bush. Otchum is dead.

He died as leader of the pack, in a fight – killed by the other dogs, who had banded together because none of them was able to take him on alone.

Nature is not a fairy tale, and sometimes it is unjust.

Soon before his demise, Otchum sired his youngest son, Carmacks, who looks like the spitting image of him. He will be the lead dog just like his father.

In the meantime Voulk is fulfilling that role.

As for Otchum, he is to be found everywhere – in every country we traveled through together, in every blizzard we confronted, with the bear, with Montaine, in every page of this story that I have written with him in the lands that made a man of me.

Acknowledgements

The expedition described in this book, across the Rocky Mountains and along the Yukon, just like all the others carried out by Otchum's family, was achieved with the assistance of Pedigree Pal. The food researched and manufactured by its engineers contributed to the success of all these adventures. I also thank Unisabi for the confidence they have shown and have continued to show.

The Siberian expedition was achieved with the support of the Painault Group.

It was with the assistance of Air Canada that we were able to travel and transport the dogs to the Rockies, then to Quebec and in the near future to Alaska.

The photographs were taken with the assistance of Leica, without whom they could not have been taken, especially at –75°F (–60°C) in the depths of the Siberian winter.